SLINGING MUD

SLINGING MUD

RUDE NICKNAMES,
SCURRILOUS SLOGANS,
and
INSULTING SLANG
from Two Centuries of
AMERICAN POLITICS

ROSEMARIE OSTLER

A PERIGEE BOOK

A PERIGEE BOOK
Published by the Penguin Group
Penguin Group (USA) Inc.
375 Hudson Street, New York, New York 10014, USA

Penguin Group (Canada), 90 Eglinton Avenue East, Suite 700, Toronto, Ontario M4P 2Y3, Canada
(a division of Pearson Penguin Canada Inc.)
Penguin Books Ltd., 80 Strand, London WC2R 0RL, England
Penguin Group Ireland, 25 St. Stephen's Green, Dublin 2, Ireland (a division of Penguin Books Ltd.)
Penguin Group (Australia), 250 Camberwell Road, Camberwell, Victoria 3124, Australia
(a division of Pearson Australia Group Pty. Ltd.)
Penguin Books India Pvt. Ltd., 11 Community Centre, Panchsheel Park, New Delhi—110 017, India
Penguin Group (NZ), 67 Apollo Drive, Rosedale, Auckland 0632, New Zealand
(a division of Pearson New Zealand Ltd.)
Penguin Books (South Africa) (Pty.) Ltd., 24 Sturdee Avenue, Rosebank, Johannesburg 2196,
South Africa
Penguin Books Ltd., Registered Offices: 80 Strand, London WC2R 0RL, England

While the author has made every effort to provide accurate telephone numbers and Internet addresses at
the time of publication, neither the publisher nor the author assumes any responsibility for errors or for
changes that occur after publication. Further, the publisher does not have any control over and does not
assume any responsibility for author or third-party websites or their content.

Copyright © 2011 by Rosemarie Ostler
Text design by Tiffany Estreicher

First edition: September 2011

Library of Congress Cataloging-in-Publication Data

Ostler, Rosemarie.
    Slinging mud : rude nicknames, scurrilous slogans, and insulting slang from two centuries of American
politics / Rosemarie Ostler.
      p.   cm.
    "A Perigee book."
    Includes bibliographical references and index.
    ISBN 978-0-399-53691-5
      1. Invective—Political aspects—United States.   2. Hate speech—United States.   3. Politicians—
United States—Language.   4. English language—Political aspects—United States.
5. Communication in politics—United States.   I. Title.
    JA85.2.U6O78   2011
    320.97301'4—dc22   2011013730

PRINTED IN THE UNITED STATES OF AMERICA

10 9 8 7 6 5 4 3 2 1

Most Perigee books are available at special quantity discounts for bulk purchases for sales promotions,
premiums, fund-raising, or educational use. Special books, or book excerpts, can also be created to fit
specific needs. For details, write: Special Markets, Penguin Group (USA) Inc., 375 Hudson Street, New
York, New York 10014.

CONTENTS

PROLOGUE

Mudslinging, an American Tradition

Pundits in recent years have taken to bemoaning the loss of civility in public discourse, apparently under the impression that the political campaigns of earlier eras were conducted with utmost courtesy and decorum. Actually, mudslinging is a venerable American tradition, on a par with baseball and apple pie. Politicians have been going negative since the days of the Founding Fathers.

The early republic churned with political controversy. Although revolutionary leaders had worked together to establish an independent nation, they were often seriously at odds over how to run it. By the time George Washington became the first president in 1788, sharply divided political factions were already forming. The Federalist faction believed in a strong central government run by the qualified few. The Republicans, also called Democratic-Republicans, supported a more participatory democracy and kept a lookout for any governmental drift toward monarchy. (Eighteenth-century Republicans are unconnected with the modern Republican Party, which was founded in the 1850s.)

Republicans scathingly referred to the Federalists as

Monocrats—monarchists in Democrats' clothing. Federalists returned the favor by smearing the Republicans as Jacobins, the radical instigators of the French Revolution. Then, as now, each side was convinced that their opponents were irresponsible lunatics whose deeply flawed policies would destroy the country.

Even George Washington had his detractors. Washington disapproved of political parties and tried to keep his administration nonpartisan, but privately he leaned toward Federalism. His chief attacker was the ferocious anti-Federalist Benjamin Franklin Bache, editor of the *Philadelphia Aurora*. Bache wrote stinging editorials accusing the president of behaving imperiously and living like an aristocrat. He considered Washington unfit for his job. One 1795 issue of the *Aurora* approvingly published a letter that described him as having "a mind unadorned by extraordinary features or uncommon capacity."

In those days, newspapers made no pretense of neutrality. They supported one side or the other and published frankly partisan editorials. Like-minded readers contributed letters to the editor, blasting political enemies under cover of classical pseudonyms such as Valerius, Atticus, and Scipio. During Washington's eight years in office, the *Aurora* and other anti-Federalist newspapers called him a cheapskate, a horse beater, a gambler, a tyrannical monster, a crocodile, a hyena, a spoiled child, and a most horrid swearer and blasphemer, among other epithets. "Retire immediately," demanded an incensed *Aurora* reader in a September 20, 1795, letter. Signing himself *Scipio*, he told Washington, "You are utterly incapable to steer the political ship."

Elections in the early United States did not involve the kind of mass campaigning that modern Americans expect. Most people couldn't vote—that privilege was reserved for white male property owners—so broad-based campaigns were pointless. Besides, openly seeking public office was considered ungentlemanly. Those in the running for a post were supposed to stay at home until the voting was over and act surprised when a messenger arrived with the news that they'd won.

Candidates didn't make stump speeches or appear at rallies. They left the electioneering to their supporters, who attacked opponents mainly through the printed word. In spite of these limitations, the 1800 presidential contest between Republican Thomas Jefferson and Federalist incumbent president John Adams managed to be one of the dirtiest on record—a verbal bloodbath fully worthy of the most negative modern campaign.

Jefferson's enthusiasm for the recent French Revolution drove Federalists into a frenzy of hysterical rhetoric. In a flood of editorials and pamphlets, they accused him of being an apostle of anarchy, a demagogue, a trickster, and a Franco-maniac. Envisioning an American Reign of Terror, the Federalist editor of the *Connecticut Courant* asked readers, "Are you prepared to see your dwellings in flames, . . . female chastity violated, or children writhing on the pike?" Another editorial warned, "Murder, robbery, rape, adultery, and incest will all be openly taught . . . the soil will be soaked with blood, and the nation black with crimes."

Jefferson's Deist beliefs also inspired attacks. "God and a religious president; . . . or Jefferson—and no God!!!!" cried the *Ga-*

zette of the United States. People were told that their Bibles would be confiscated if Jefferson were elected.

Jefferson's private life came under scrutiny. Whispers circulated about his *Congo harem,* meaning the female slaves on his Virginia plantation. One Federalist handbill claimed Jefferson himself was part black. It described him as "a mean-spirited, low-lived fellow, . . . sired by a Virginia mulatto father . . . raised wholly on hoe-cake . . . , bacon and hominy, with an occasional change of fricasseed bullfrog."

The attacks were not all from one side. Republicans lambasted John Adams as an unprincipled warmonger because the American navy had been skirmishing with the French. They accused him of having delusions of grandeur, spreading the rumor that he planned to marry off one of his sons to a daughter of George III and found an Anglo-American dynasty. The tale went that Adams abandoned his plot only when George Washington came to his office wearing a revolutionary uniform and brandishing a sword.

A Republican pamphlet called "The Prospect Before Us" accused Adams of election fraud in 1796 and "multiple corruptions" since then. The pamphleteer also attacked his famously hot temper: "The reign of Mr. Adams has been one continued tempest of malignant passions." The Republicans also circulated the unlikely story that Adams had sent his running mate, Charles Pinckney, to England to procure four girls as mistresses, two for Pinckney and two for himself. When Adams heard the story, he humorously remarked that Pinckney must have "kept them all for himself and cheated me out of my two."

Fellow Federalist Alexander Hamilton, who would have preferred Pinckney as president, struck a more devastating blow. In a lengthy open letter to party members he complained of "the disgusting egotism, distempered jealousy and ungovernable indiscretion of Mr. Adams's temper." He added, "I should be deficient in candor were I to conceal the conviction that he does not possess the talents adapted to the Administration of Government." Hamilton meant the letter for Federalists only, but Jefferson's running mate Aaron Burr acquired a copy and had it published in the newspapers—a coup comparable to posting a leaked video clip on YouTube.

Hamilton's "thunderbolt," as the Republicans called it, was not the deciding factor in making Adams a one-term president, but it undoubtedly helped. Jefferson won the election, and Adams retired to his Massachusetts farm, the first candidate—but hardly the last—to be done in by mud flung from both directions.

And so it has gone ever since. The 1800 election set the tone for future political battles. Two hundred years ago attacks were spread with hand-printed pamphlets distributed door-to-door. Today they take the form of thirty-second sound bites going viral on the Internet. Still, style and content have held remarkably steady over time. Charges of corruption, incompetence, warmongering, elitism, stupidity, immorality, lack of patriotism, wasting public money—the details change with each election cycle, but the themes remain the same.

This book takes a look at two centuries' worth of memorable mudslinging, starting with the first wide-scale campaign, the bitter 1824 battle between John Quincy Adams and Andrew Jackson. It ends with the 2008 presidential contest between John

McCain and Barack Obama. That no-holds-barred event proved that mudslinging can still take new twists, even after all these years.

In between, readers will discover a choice collection of rude slogans, scandalous rumors, insulting labels, over-the-top personal attacks, and lowdown slurs from every American era. Highly colorful, frequently inaccurate, always brutal—these words and phrases capture the unique flavor of politics in the United States.

★ 1 ★

King Mob

THE JACKSONIAN ERA

1824–1848

Full-bore campaigning arrived in the 1820s. Until then, politics had been run by the propertied upper classes. Even theoretical radicals like Thomas Jefferson came from aristocratic backgrounds. Things changed when Tennessee, Kentucky, Ohio, and other frontier states were admitted to the Union. These states gave voting rights to all white men, regardless of economic status. Partly to discourage their citizens from moving west, most of the original thirteen states eventually broadened their voter base as well.

Along with votes for the common man came a whole new level of attack campaigning. Scurrilous pamphlets and flyers were widely distributed, and large broadsides were posted on walls and fences. While the candidates themselves stayed in the background, supporters gave rabble-rousing stump speeches, followed by drinks all around at the nearest tavern. Personal attacks rose to new levels and no subject was off-limits.

1824

JOHN Q. ADAMS VS. ANDREW JACKSON VS. WILLIAM CRAWFORD VS. HENRY CLAY (DEMOCRATIC-REPUBLICANS)

The Corrupt Bargain

Four leading contenders ran for the presidency in 1824—all from the Democratic-Republican Party, but with support from different party factions. (Partywide nominating conventions were not held until 1832.) Party insiders favored William Crawford of Georgia, a longtime senator and cabinet member; John Quincy Adams of Massachusetts, son of John Adams, was popular in New England; longtime legislator Henry Clay of Kentucky was strong in the South and West; Andrew Jackson of Tennessee was the people's candidate. Jackson had little government experience, and his stands on the issues were cloudy, but he was the Hero of New Orleans during the War of 1812 and a famous Indian fighter. Jackson was the choice of men who wanted to vote for someone like themselves—the nineteenth-century equivalent of a candidate voters could imagine having a beer with.

None of the contenders in 1824 won a majority of the electoral votes. Andrew Jackson received the most, as well as the highest number of popular votes. Adams came in second. Lack of a majority meant the House of Representatives would decide the election. Clay, who had finished last and had no hope of winning, threw his influence behind Adams, guaranteeing him the presidency.

Jackson supporters were furious, especially when Adams appointed Clay secretary of state shortly after the election. One typically outraged newspaper comment took the style of an obituary: "Expired at Washington . . . of poison administered at the assassin hands of John Quincy Adams, the usurper, and Henry Clay, the virtue, liberty, and independence of the United States." Jacksonians began shouting about a "corrupt bargain." They accused Clay of selling his votes in exchange for a position in the cabinet.

Clay insisted that no deal had been struck. In fact, his support of Adams was predictable. The two men shared many political views, and Clay made it clear during the campaign that he didn't like Jackson. Alluding to Jackson's win at the Battle of New Orleans, Clay wrote to a friend that he could not believe that killing twenty-five thousand Englishmen qualified Jackson "for the various, difficult and complicated duties of the Chief Magistracy." Adams's choice of the experienced Clay as secretary of state was also unsurprising.

Jackson and his supporters remained unappeased. They kept up a continuous battle cry of "corrupt bargain" for the next four years, starting the 1828 campaign against Adams even before he entered the White House. And it worked—Jackson got elected the next time around.

The term *corrupt bargain* has been hauled out of storage occasionally since Jackson's time to mean "political collusion for mutual benefit." One occasion was the election of Rutherford B. Hayes in 1876. Hayes informally agreed to withdraw Union troops from certain southern states in return for their electoral votes (see Chapter 3).

1828

ANDREW JACKSON (DEMOCRAT) VS. JOHN Q. ADAMS (NATIONAL REPUBLICAN)

The ABC of Democracy

The 1828 campaign reached new heights of political vituperation. The Democratic-Republican Party split, with Jacksonians now known simply as Democrats and Adams supporters as National Republicans. The Democrats constantly reminded voters of the corrupt bargain that had stolen the presidency from Jackson in 1824. They attacked Adams as an aristocrat who lived in "kingly pomp and splendor," a secret monarchist, and an old-school Federalist in disguise. They accused him of authorizing extravagant expenditures while president.

Although Adams was known to be straitlaced, Jackson supporters claimed he lived an irreligious lifestyle. They implied that his choice of church—Unitarian—was unorthodox and suspect compared with Jackson's straightforward Presbyterianism. They referred to the White House billiards table and a chess set as a "gaming table" and "gambling furniture." Most ludicrous, they claimed that Adams, while a minister to Russia, had procured a young American girl for the entertainment of Czar Alexander I.

Finally, in an attack with modern overtones, Democrats criticized Adams for being too educated. With Jackson in the White House, his supporters claimed, Americans would not be forced to listen to "painful struggles after eloquence."

The Adams campaign's attacks on Jackson were even more virulent and personal. Following in the gentlemanly tradition of his father and other early presidents, Adams himself did not campaign. However, he didn't stop his supporters from throwing mud with both hands. Their main target was Jackson's personal history. One Adamsite published an eight-page pamphlet detailing Jackson's "youthful indiscretions," including fourteen alleged duels, brawls, and shoot-outs.

Another attack took aim at Jackson's reputation as the Hero of New Orleans. John Binns, editor of the *Philadelphia Democratic Press*, printed a poster accusing Jackson of murder in the case of six militiamen who were convicted as deserters during the War of 1812 and executed. Titled "Some Account of Some of the Bloody Deeds of General Jackson," it featured a drawing of six coffins with the name of an executed man written above each.

The story, supposedly based on an eyewitness report, claimed the militiamen were temporary replacements who had volunteered for three months only. Believing that their time was up, they attempted to leave for home. The handbill then described the scene of execution, including an account of how the men were ordered to stand in front of their own coffins before being shot down by firing squads of fellow soldiers.

The Jackson campaign tried to counteract this tale, explaining that the convicted soldiers had broken into a warehouse and stolen supplies, among other crimes, before deserting. When captured they received fair trials. Adams supporters shrugged off this explanation and continued to insist that Jackson was a murderer. Binns eventually printed several anti-Jackson posters that are sometimes collectively referred to as "The Coffin Handbills."

The most vicious smear was against Jackson's wife, Rachel. Rachel had been married to a man named Lewis Robards, who left her in 1790 with the understanding that he would obtain a divorce. Thinking she was free, Rachel married Jackson in 1791. In fact, Robards had delayed filing. The Jacksons discovered to their horror in 1794 that Rachel's divorce decree had only recently become official. They immediately remarried.

The Republicans latched onto Rachel's "bigamy" as a major campaign issue. Adams supporters marched with banners carrying the slogan "The A B C of Democracy / The Adulteress / The Bully / And the Cuckold." Anti-Jackson newspapers also expressed their outrage. The *Cincinnati Gazette* published a pamphlet asking, "Ought a convicted adulteress and her paramour husband to be placed in the highest offices of this free and Christian land?" The true explanation of Rachel's marital situation was less compelling than the story circulated by Jackson's enemies, but, then as now, sex sold.

Although *King Mob* is now associated with the Jacksonian era, Justice Story did not invent the term. It had been a way to describe the uncontrolled masses since the eighteenth century. Labeling a powerful trend or person "king" was common. A similar example is *King Cotton*, shorthand for the economic importance of cotton in the pre–Civil War South.

The scandal did not ultimately prevent Jackson from being elected. However, Rachel Jackson, who suffered from heart trouble, died a few days before the inauguration. Jackson blamed her death on stress caused by the Republican campaign attacks. Visiting her tomb shortly after her funeral, he said, "May God forgive her murderers as I know she forgave them! I never can!"

King Mob

When Jackson won the presidency in 1828, his opponents complained that he would bring degradation on the office of the president with his uncouth ways. They felt vindicated by the events of inauguration day. During the postinaugural reception, a throng of excited Jackson supporters streamed into the White House, muddying carpets and trampling furniture, standing on chairs in their dirty boots to get a better view, and smashing glass and china in their mad scramble to get at the refreshments. Men, women, and children of every class and description were so tightly packed into the public rooms that they seemed in danger of bursting out the windows. Supreme Court justice Joseph Story, an aghast witness, records, "I never saw such a mixture. The reign of King Mob seemed triumphant." The chaos was only relieved somewhat when the punch and lemonade were poured into buckets and carried out onto the lawn, followed by thirsty partiers.

Fence Sitters, Pettifoggers, and Logrollers

The belief that Congress was full of insiders and men on the make strengthened during the 1820s. Several derogatory terms for legislative activities gained popularity during this time.

One that's still popular is *fence sitter* to mean "a waffler," or someone waiting to see how events develop. An early use appears in an 1829 magazine story titled "Scenes in Washington." The narrator wryly describes "the Honourable Mr. Spratt," who "having been elected to Congress for no political reason, but on some local question, . . . was 'on the fence,' where, like a wise man he determined to sit, until he had made up his mind on which side it would be most pleasant and profitable for him to get off." The label *fence sitter* still implies that a legislator lacks firm principles and moral courage.

A less common word today is *pettifogger*. The word originally meant a lawyer who dealt with petty, or trivial, cases. By the eighteenth century it evolved to mean a crooked lawyer or one who quibbled over small points. An early political example of the word comes from the *New-Hampshire Patriot*, a newspaper that supported Jackson. Referring to attacks by the Adams campaign, the editor says that Adams supporter Henry Clay is behaving "like a shyster, pettifogging in a . . . [law]suit." The word is occasionally used in modern times, as in this remark in a 1992 *Economist* article:

"Without lifetime careers to preserve, congressmen would be free to debate and discuss rather than pettifog and pander."

Although the word *logrolling* is now rarely heard, the practice itself—agreeing to vote for someone's pet project if that person will vote for yours—is still well entrenched. Logrolling literally meant the frontier tradition of getting together to clear land of excess timber. The resulting logs were usually rolled into a pile and burned. Because logrolling required several people, neighbors were expected to take turns helping each other. At a time when many Americans were clearing previously unfarmed land, they would easily have understood the collaborative implications of legislative logrolling.

Bunkum

The folks of Buncombe County, North Carolina, had a conscientious representative in Felix Walker. During an 1820 debate on the Missouri question—whether Missouri should be admitted to the Union as a free or slave state—Walker rose at the end of the day and began a rambling speech. When impatient colleagues pleaded with him to stop, pointing out that no one was listening, he replied, "Never mind; I'm talking to Buncombe." Representative Walker's main purpose was not to achieve legislative action, but to show his constituents back home that he was fulfilling his duties.

Buncombe, usually written with the simplified spelling *bunkum*, soon took on the meaning of empty political oratory—talk for the sake of talking. It was shortened to *bunk* in the twentieth century. *Debunk*, meaning "to remove the bunk from a statement," was in use by the 1920s.

1832

ANDREW JACKSON (DEMOCRAT) VS. HENRY CLAY (NATIONAL REPUBLICAN)

King Andrew I

The 1832 campaign was short on compelling issues. That partly explains why the election's main controversy centered around the usually staid topic of banks—specifically, the Bank of the United States. This privately owned, for-profit institution handled the federal government's finances and controlled the amount of paper money that state banks could issue. To Henry Clay and like-minded Republicans it was a stabilizing financial force for good. To President Andrew Jackson, on the other hand, it was a "mammoth monopoly" and a "hydra of corruption."

Believing that most voters respected the bank as much as he did, Republican candidate Clay decided to challenge Jackson on the issue. He persuaded the bank's president, Nicholas Biddle, to ask Congress for a charter renewal before the election, even though the bank's charter did not actually expire until 1836. Unfortunately for his election chances, Clay had seriously misread the public mood.

Jackson successfully vetoed the renewal bill, on the grounds that the bank was an antidemocratic institution devoted to making "the rich richer and the powerful more potent." Far from reacting with outrage, rank-and-file voters—the Great Unwashed, as Biddle called them—cheered the president's stand. They saw the veto as a blow against the forces of economic elitism.

The Republicans tried to save the situation by arguing that

Jackson had thwarted the will of the people, or at least the will of their congressional representatives. They nicknamed the president King Andrew I. "The King upon the throne: the people in the dust!!!" shouted one headline. Another newspaper declared Jackson "the most absolute despot now at the head of any representative government." Cartoons portrayed him wearing a crown and an ermine-trimmed cape.

The Democrats made a few mild attacks on Clay—for instance, drawing attention to the fact that he occasionally gambled—but they concentrated on rallying the voters with pro-Jackson parades and other entertainments. It was a wise strategy. In spite of his opponents' attacks and with little effort on his part, Jackson remained overwhelmingly popular. Weeks before Election Day he assured his friend Isaac Hill, "It'll be a walk." His confidence was justified. He won reelection by a large margin, garnering almost twice as many votes as Clay.

1836

Martin Van Buren (Democrat) vs. Four Whig Candidates

Sweet Sandy Whiskers

In 1836 Martin Van Buren narrowly won the presidency against four candidates from the Whig Party, recently organized by former National Republicans. Although united in their hatred of the Jackson administration, the Whigs were unable to rally behind a national candidate. Instead, they nominated men popular in various regions.

Van Buren's Whig opponents attacked him in various ways. They denigrated him as illiterate, saying in campaign flyers that his "mind beats round, like a tame bear tied to a stake, in a little circle, hardly bigger than the circumference of the head in which it is placed." They claimed he was a "dandy," prim and fussy about his appearance. They accused him of wearing corsets and called him Sweet Sandy Whiskers because he scented his reddish whiskers.

He was labeled the Little Magician and the Red Fox of Kinderhook (the New York town where he was born) to highlight what his enemies saw as slipperiness and lack of principle. They also coined the adjective *vanburenish* to describe someone who is evasive or uncommitted in politics. David Crockett, a former congressman who supported fellow Tennessean Hugh White, wrote about Van Buren, "It is said that at a year old he could laugh on one side of his face and cry on the other, at one and the same time."

Although the Van Buren campaign took a few negative swipes at the Whigs, they concentrated on organizing the voters and keeping party members loyal. Van Buren received less than 51 percent of the vote, indicating that he was not overwhelmingly popular, but Whig support was too scattered for any one candidate to gain an edge.

Loco-Focos

The Democrats were increasingly torn by factions in the 1830s and 1840s. Pro-Jackson New York Democrats organized the Equal Rights Party in 1835. Equal Righters were against monopolies, a national bank, and paper money and in favor of unions, gold and silver currency, and equal rights for all. Their opponents were the conservative supporters of the Tammany Society, long the linch-pin of Democratic machine politics in New York.

The Equal Righters won the nickname of Loco-Foco after a memorable 1835 meeting held at Tammany Hall to nominate local candidates for the upcoming election. Both factions of the party, hoping to dominate the meeting, congregated early outside the hall. As soon as the doors opened, members of the Equal Rights Party burst through the front door and rushed up the stairs to the meeting room, while the Tammanies charged up the back stairs.

In the ensuing chaos, the gas lamps that lit the meeting room were extinguished. However, the Equal Righters—apparently warned ahead of time that the Tammanies might use this ploy to break up the meeting—had come prepared. They carried recently patented self-igniting matches, known by the brand name "Loco-Foco." Lighting these up, they called the meeting to order. The Tammany slate eventually triumphed, but only after much force-ful argument from their Equal Rights opponents.

When newspapers heard about the evening's rumpus, they immediately dubbed the Equal Righters Loco-Focos. The Whigs then started using *Loco-Foco* as a derogatory nickname for the entire Democratic Party, implying that all Democrats were "loco," or crazy. (The name of the matches probably comes from the Span-ish words for *crazy* and *fire*—*loco* and *fuego*.)

Enemies of the Equal Rights Party gave them other nicknames as well, including Disorganizers, Intruders, Rowdies, Eleventh Hour Democrats, Pests of Party, Infidels, Resolution Mongers, and several names that allude to the match-lighting episode— Fireflies of Faction, Jack o' Lanterns who shine in an unhealthy atmosphere, Small Lights, and the Guy Fawkeses of Politics. The Equal Rights Party dissolved at the end of the 1840s.

Slang-Whangers and Wire-Pullers

The nickname *slang-whanger* for a politician who engages in noisy rants began appearing during the 1830s. David Crockett's 1837 autobiography *Col. Crockett's Exploits and Adventures in Texas* features an early example of the term. Describing an encounter with a Van Buren supporter, Crockett says, "He talked loud, which is the way with all politicians educated in the Jackson school; and by his slang-whanging drew a considerable crowd around us."

The origin of the word *slang* is mysterious. It has been part of English since around 1750, first as a term for low, vulgar language, then expanding to cover any kind of colloquial speech. In the nineteenth century, *slang* was sometimes used as a label for nonsensical talk. It could also denote abusive language. For example, a shouted argument—what modern Americans might call a *shouting match*— was called a *slanging match*. Calling politicians slang-whangers suggested that their public speeches amounted to either nonsense or verbal abuse, or maybe both. The word continued to be used into the 1890s.

While the slang-whangers made public stump speeches, the wire-pullers worked behind the scenes. This term also began appearing in print in the 1830s, with the meaning of a political intriguer. The obvious reference is to pulling the strings of marionettes.

Wire-pullers could be insiders who worked quietly to further the interests of their party or their faction of it, as in this quotation from the *New York Mirror* of June 5, 1848, describing the Whig nominating convention: "The Philadelphia Convention will assemble on Wednesday; already that city is filled with wire-pullers, public opinion manufacturers, . . . and the whole brood of political makeshifts." Wire-pullers could also be constituents powerful enough to unseat an incumbent, as in this statement by a legislator that appeared in the January 26, 1847, *Congressional Globe*: "Neither by demonstrations here, nor by figuring and wirepulling at home, am I engaged to the support of this bill." The word was still occasionally heard in the twentieth century.

1840

William Henry Harrison (Whig) vs. Martin Van Buren (Democrat)

Old Tip-ler Against Martin Van Ruin

By 1840 the Whigs had learned a few campaigning tricks from the Democrats. To run against incumbent Martin Van Buren, they nominated a candidate with crowd appeal—one who, at least superficially, resembled the original "people's candidate," Andrew Jackson. Unlike Jackson, William Henry Harrison did not actually come from a rugged frontier background. He owned a prosperous two-thousand-acre Ohio farm with a sixteen-room house. Also unlike Jackson, Harrison's military record was undistinguished.

However, he had led the 1811 Battle of Tippecanoe against members of Tecumseh's pan-Indian confederacy, allowing his supporters to dub him Tippecanoe Harrison. When John Tyler of Virginia joined the ticket, they created arguably the most memorable campaign slogan in American history: "Tippecanoe and Tyler too!"

The Harrison campaign's most inspired idea was to adopt a Democratic opponent's insult as their campaign theme. A letter to the editor published in the *Baltimore Republican* suggested a way to put an end to Harrison's run for president: "Give him a barrel of hard cider and settle a pension of $2,000 a year on him, and my word for it, he will sit the remainder of his days in his log cabin."

The Whigs seized joyfully on this somewhat inaccurate image of Harrison as a simple rustic man who drank hard cider—comparable to a modern politician drinking cheap beer from a can. They believed they could capture the same voters who had shown so much enthusiasm for Andrew Jackson in 1828. Harrison's run for president became known as "The hard cider and log cabin campaign."

Harrison was the first to turn a presidential campaign into a full-blown circus. Party stalwarts threw huge barbecues, complete with bottomless barrels of hard cider. They staged parades that featured floats carrying log cabins. They wore coonskin caps at rallies and sang "The Log Cabin Song" and "Old Tip and the Log Cabin Boys." Whig journals sprang into being with names like *The Log Cabin Farmer*, *The Log Cabin Rifle*, and *The Log Cabin Advocate*.

A frenzy of merchandising produced campaign-related items ranging from Tippecanoe shaving soap to Tippecanoe handkerchiefs. The E. C. Booz distillery began producing log cabin–shaped bottles of whiskey. These novelty items probably helped popularize *booze* as a slang word for liquor. The Harrison campaign also popularized the expression *keep the ball rolling*. Campaigners rolled ten-foot-high slogan-covered parade balls through the streets of towns across the country, shouting to the crowds to "keep the ball rolling" for the Whig ticket.

The Democrats tried to counteract this positive image. They nicknamed Harrison Old Tip-ler and created verses like this one: "Hush a-bye-baby / Daddy's a Whig / Before he comes home / Hard cider he'll swig; / Then he'll be tipsy and over he'll fall; / Down will come Daddy, Tip, Tyler and all." They also attacked the sixty-eight-year-old Harrison as senile and incoherent and accused him of using "shocking profanity."

Democrats claimed that Harrison had cohabited with Native American women out on the Ohio frontier. Worst of all, they attacked his record as the Hero of Tippecanoe, pointing out that he had retired from the army a year before the War of 1812 ended. Democrats invented yet another nickname to suggest a lack of manliness—Granny Harrison, the Petticoat General.

The Whigs also did some mudslinging. Representative Charles Ogle of Pennsylvania gave a floor speech that was later reprinted under the title "The Regal Splendor of the President's Palace." On the pretext of questioning a government request for $3,665 (equal to about $80,000 now) to make improvements and repairs to the White House, Ogle accused President Van Buren of living in high style on the taxpayers' money. He gave listeners a tour of the presidential palace, describing "its spacious courts, its gorgeous banqueting halls, its . . . gilt chandeliers." He claimed that congressmen dining with the president had been fed rich dishes with French-ified names and "the choicest brands" of champagne, burgundy, and other wines. (No hard cider for Van Buren!) Ogle wrapped up his speech by stating that he was unwilling to vote for the appropriation in question because he feared it would be spent "for the purchase of a crown, diadem, sceptre, and royal jewels."

The speech was an absurd misrepresentation of Van Buren's life in the White House. Nonetheless, it served its purpose of instilling in voters' minds an image of Van Buren as a self-indulgent aristocrat, in contrast to the more down-to-earth Harrison. Van Buren's supposed wastefulness, coupled with a struggling economy, led to a new nickname—Martin Van Ruin.

The Whigs wrote anti–Van Buren verses along the same lines: "Ole Tip, he wears a homespun shirt, / He has no ruffled shirt, wirt, wirt / But Matt he has the golden plate / And he's a little squirt, wirt, wirt" (a slap at Van Buren's small stature).

Democrats irritably pointed out that Harrison, as a clerk of the court, enjoyed a $6,000 a year income and lived not in a log cabin, but in a fine large house. In a complaint that has since become familiar, they also accused the Whigs of indulging in frivolities instead of addressing serious campaign issues. The Democratic newspaper the *Pennsylvanian* complained, "We speak of the divorce of bank and state; and the Whigs reply with a dissertation on the merits of hard cider." Van Buren supporters labeled Harrison General Mum because, at the advice of his campaign organizers, he avoided taking specific positions on issues.

Voters turned out to be less interested in the details of Harrison's platform than in the excitement of rallying around a popular figure. Many people were also angry with Van Buren, who was blamed for the economic hard times of the late 1830s. With a voter turnout of around 80 percent, Harrison won overwhelmingly.

Whig exuberance was short-lived. Harrison contracted pneumonia shortly after the inauguration and one month later he was dead. The voters who had rallied so strongly for Tippecanoe were left with Tyler, a former Democrat who changed parties because he didn't like Jackson.

Tyler soon showed that his political sympathies remained with the Democrats. He went against the Whig Party's commitment to a protective tariff and a strong national government in favor of supporting Democratic Party principles of free trade and states' rights. While still president, Tyler was drummed out of the Whig Party and his Whig cabinet resigned. He replaced them with Democrats.

Bloviate

Bloviate, meaning "to make lengthy speeches full of high-flown rhetoric," first arose as a political term around the 1840s. An early use is found in the *Norwalk (OH) Huron Reflector* for October 14, 1845: "Peter P. Low, Esq., will with open throat . . . bloviate about the farmers being taxed upon the full value of their farms, while the bankers are released from taxation." The word seems to have been especially popular in Ohio and may have originated there. It is almost certainly related to another term that was current in the mid-nineteenth century, *blower*, to mean "a noisy, talkative person or a boaster." *Blowhard* also comes from this meaning of *blow*. The words *bloviator* and *bloviation* were part of the language by the 1870s.

Bloviate went obsolete by the late nineteenth century, but was revived during Warren Harding's 1920 run for the presidency. Harding confessed that he liked to bloviate, using the word in the sense of chatting or shooting the breeze. Many people thought *bloviate* in its "speechify" sense was an ideal way to describe Harding's own convoluted campaign speeches, complete with odd words like *normalcy*. (For more about Harding, see Chapter 4.)

Bloviate is once again popular as an insulting way to describe political speech. It appears frequently in newspaper opinion pieces and blog sites. For instance, in a December 31, 2008, opinion piece posted on the ABC News website, reporter John Stossel remarked, "Senators bloviate on anything and everything."

1844

JAMES POLK (DEMOCRAT) VS. HENRY CLAY (WHIG)

Polk the Plodder

James K. Polk was the Democrats' dark horse in 1844. Although the Tennessean had been Speaker of the House between 1835 and 1839, he was relatively unknown to the general public. His tenure as Speaker was so colorless that some congressmen called him Polk the Plodder. The party faithful greeted Polk's nomination with incredulity. They were puzzled over what this nonentity had done to be chosen over more illustrious candidates such as Martin Van Buren. His Whig opponents adopted the slogan "Who Is James K. Polk?"

Polk was nominated because he took a popular position on the most divisive question of the day—whether the independent republic of Texas, where slavery was legal, should be annexed to the United States. Northerners opposed to slavery were against admitting such a large slaveholding region into the Union, while southerners were ardently in favor of it. Martin Van Buren, the obvious choice for the Democratic presidential nomination, was firmly opposed to annexation. Southern Democrats therefore refused to accept him as a candidate, telling the nominating committee that the northern states could name their man, as long as it wasn't Van Buren.

Not only did Polk believe Texas ought to be annexed, he was enthusiastically in favor of pushing the boundaries of the Oregon

Territory as far north as 54°40' latitude, or what is now the middle of British Columbia. The Democrats campaigned with the rallying cry, "All of Texas, all of Oregon!" The snappier slogan "Fifty-four forty or fight!" actually appeared after the election. (The United States eventually agreed to a compromise boundary at the 49th parallel.)

Democrats went heavily negative against the Whig candidate, Henry Clay, who was making another run for the presidency. They circulated a pamphlet titled "Twenty-one Reasons Why Clay Should Not Be Elected," accusing him of drinking brandy, fighting duels, and visiting brothels, as well as reviving the gambling charges of 1832. Another flyer blared the warning, "Christian Voters! Read, Pause and Reflect! Mr. Clay's Moral Character." Clay did enjoy drinking and gambling, as did many Americans, but did neither to excess.

Clay lost narrowly to Polk, but aspersions on his moral character were not the cause. As a Whig, Clay was in a trickier position than Polk. While the Democrats overwhelmingly supported the annexation of Texas, northern and southern Whigs were divided on the issue. Faced with the difficult challenge of keeping both wings of the party happy, Clay vacillated.

Clay originally announced that he was opposed to "immediate annexation" of Texas, but as the campaign progressed, his position softened. Then, when he realized he was losing his northern voters, he backtracked and announced that he was "decidedly opposed" to annexation. In the end, he alienated voters on both sides of the question. The connected issues of westward expansion and slavery would increasingly cause problems for the Whigs.

1848

Zachary Taylor (Whig) vs. Lewis Cass (Democrat) vs. Martin Van Buren (Free Soil)

Economical, Comical Old Zach

In 1848 the Whigs once again nominated a war hero—career military man Zachary Taylor. General Taylor caught the popular imagination because his army division fought the first battles of the Mexican War that came about when the United States annexed Texas in 1845. Otherwise, Taylor was an odd choice at first glance. He had no political experience and claimed never to have voted. However, the Whigs considered his lack of a record an advantage—they could sidestep serious political discussions and concentrate on Taylor's hero status. Admirers called him Old Rough and Ready and formed Old Rough and Ready Clubs around the country to support his campaign.

The Democrats ridiculed Taylor as Economical, Comical Old Zach. When the war ended, Taylor had returned to his home in Baton Rouge. After receiving several letters with insufficient postage, he told the Baton Rouge postmaster to send all unpaid mail to the dead letter office. Rumor had it that the letter offering him the nomination languished there for weeks. Eventually, the Whig nominating committee was forced to send another letter, postage fully prepaid. The Democrats used this anecdote, as well as Taylor's shabby way of dressing, as evidence that he was cheap.

Overall, however, the 1848 campaign was short on colorful

nicknames and slogans. Although the conflict over slavery was building, both major parties managed to avoid taking any firm stand. Those committed to ending slavery formed the Free Soil Party, whose candidate, former president Van Buren, drew a significant number of votes from the Democrats. This drain on Cass's voting base, along with Taylor's popularity as a general, was enough to allow Taylor to win by a slim margin.

Barnburners and Hunkers

The rise of Barnburners and Hunkers, two offshoots of New York's Democratic Party, reflects the growing importance of slavery as a national issue in the late 1840s. Barnburners were the party's radicals who, among other beliefs, opposed extending slavery into the country's western territories. They received their nickname from a Tammany Hall member who said, "These men are incendiaries; they are mad; they are like the farmer, who, to get the rats out of his granary, sets fire to his own barn." He was referring to a familiar joke in which an old Dutch farmer sets fire to his barn to chase out the rats. (Slurs against the original Dutch settlers were common in New York. The term *Dutch treat* to mean "a 'treat' that you pay for yourself" is another example.)

Barnburners did in fact inflict some damage on the Democratic Party. The Free Soil Party, which contributed to the Democrats' defeat in 1848, consisted mostly of Barnburners angry over the Democrats' stand on slavery in the territories. Their candidate, Martin Van Buren, although never in serious contention, drew enough votes to make the Democrats lose.

In the 1930s, long after the barn-burning Democrats were forgotten, the term *barn burner* became popular as slang for an excitingly positive thing, such as an exceptionally good bridge hand. Joseph Bryon's World War II memoir, *Aircraft Carrier*, includes the line: "The cards loved us; we held one barn burner after the other."

The Hunkers, sometimes called Old Hunkers, were the opposite of radical. They did not have strong feelings about slavery, considering the issue no business of New York's. Hunkers were more interested in hunkering down with whatever political gains they could accrue. They nearly always voted with southern Democrats for the sake of party unity and to keep their positions secure.

One possible origin of *Hunker* is the Dutch word *honk*, meaning "home base" in a game. In nineteenth-century New York, *to reach hunk* was children's slang for safely reaching home during a game of tag. Another possibility is that the label derives from a popular nineteenth-century nickname for a surly, miserly old man, Old Hunks. Either term could be extended fairly naturally to cover New York's Old Hunkers. As soon as they landed safely on their political home base, they clung tightly to whatever rewards they received.

Barnburners and Hunkers, called Softshells and Hardshells in the 1850s, were just two of the desperately opposed factions that fought for political control in the run-up to the Civil War. As the decade progressed, political positions in the North and South would become ever more at odds.

★ 2 ★

Doughfaces and Copperheads

THE ANTEBELLUM PERIOD
AND THE CIVIL WAR

1852–1868

As the country careened toward civil war, questions of slavery and secession overwhelmed other issues. Political discourse took on a harder edge, and the attacks didn't stop with name calling. In the bitter struggle over whether slavery would be legal in the western territories, hot words frequently boiled over into physical violence. Beatings and even shootings regularly occurred. In trouble spots such as Kansas, those on the losing side of an argument might be subjected to the recently revived tradition of "tarring and feathering."

In spite of the seriousness of the country's problems, political campaigns still relied on the usual disparaging nicknames and libelous innuendoes. The candidate's war record, family background, private life, personal appearance, speaking style, behavioral quirks—all were fair game for the opposition. Abraham Lincoln, now one of the most revered American presidents, was widely ridiculed for his odd looks and humble social background.

Partisan groups abounded before the war, each with its own—usually unflattering—nickname. Several negative terms for politicians that were unconnected with the conflict also entered the vocabulary during the mid-nineteenth century.

High Muckamucks

The term *high muckamuck* became popular sometime in the 1850s as a way to demonstrate a lack of awe toward powerful people. Its first appearance in print comes from the Sacramento *Democratic State Journal* for November 1, 1856: "The professors—the high 'Muck-a-Mucks'—tried [political] fusion, and produced confusion."

Muckamuck is borrowed from Chinook Jargon, a trading language in wide use among Pacific Northwest tribes during the mid-nineteenth century, when American settlers started arriving in the area. The word translates roughly as "food" or "provisions." The whole phrase may derive from *hiu muckamuck*, meaning "plenty to eat," with English speakers misinterpreting *hiu* as "high." Americans first used *muckamuck* to mean "eat," usually when writing about Native Americans. A typical example is found in writer Theodore Winthrop's 1853 letter to his mother: "We stopped once or twice for [the guides] to 'muck-a-muck.'"

By the 1860s *high muckamuck* had morphed into a common term for a big shot. The logic may be that having plenty of provisions translates into wealth and power.

Although not necessarily political, *high muckamuck* was—and is—often applied sarcastically to politicians who need to be taken down a peg. A common variation is *high muckety-muck*.

Doughfaces

A literal doughface in the nineteenth century was a mask made of dough or papier-mâché. These were sometimes worn to frighten people for a joke, and the earliest figurative uses of *doughface* carry the suggestion of a false bogeyman.

John Randolph, a Virginian who served in Congress at various times between 1799 and 1833, was probably the first to use the word politically, during a debate over the 1820 Missouri Compromise. The Compromise admitted Maine to the Union as a Free State and Missouri as a slave state. Thereafter, slavery would be prohibited in Louisiana Purchase territories north of 36°30' latitude, but allowed south of that line. Randolph, a supporter of slavery, nonetheless spoke sneeringly of Northerners willing to compromise on this issue. He said, "I knew these men would give way. They were scared at their own dough-faces." He may have meant that they spooked themselves with the specter of Southern secession.

During the 1850s, *doughface* could cover any politician who lacked loyalty to his party and region. While Northerners defined doughfaces as those who were soft on the slavery question, Southerners used the term for colleagues who didn't defend slavery staunchly enough. Both sides despised doughfaces. The *New York Tribune*, writing on June 29, 1848, about South Carolinian John C. Calhoun, says, "Desperate, idolatrous, and blind as is his devotion to slavery, we would sooner see him President to-morrow than any dough-face in the Union. He is . . . no oily wriggler." Eventually *doughface* extended to politicians whose principles were flexible on any issue, not just slavery—especially when money was involved.

1852

Franklin Pierce (Democrat) vs. Winfield Scott (Whig)

Old Fuss 'n' Feathers Challenges the Fainting General
The 1852 presidential campaign was the last one before the Civil War that didn't focus primarily on slavery. Congress staved off sectional conflict for a few more years with the Compromise of 1850. Like the earlier Missouri Compromise, this agreement was intended to maintain a balance between slave and Free States. Among other provisions, it admitted California as a Free State and allowed New Mexico and Utah to decide their own status by popular vote. Both the Whigs and the Democrats endorsed the

Compromise. This neutralized slavery as a campaign issue and allowed the candidates to focus on their opponents' personal shortcomings.

Having had good luck with the Mexican War hero Zachary Taylor in 1848, the Whigs nominated another veteran of the same war—General Winfield Scott. Unfortunately, Scott came off as more at home on the parade ground than the battlefield. His officers referred to him as Old Fuss 'n' Feathers because he liked to parade wearing his best dress uniform. The Democrats accused him of being vain and silly, and warned of a "reign of Epaulets" if he were elected.

Democrats also accused Scott of being hostile to recent immigrants. This charge was potentially serious because male immigrants were allowed to vote in most states. In response, Scott embarked on an extended campaign tour, disguised as a search for a place to build a military hospital. He needed an excuse because open campaigning was still considered undignified. Although party functionaries engaged in plenty of hard-edged electioneering, presidential candidates themselves were supposed to stay above the fray as much as possible.

Scott made fifty-two speeches during his trip. These included numerous awkward comments on the "rich Irish brogue" or "sweet German accent" of audience members and stilted reassurances that Scott welcomed "adopted citizens."

The Democratic candidate, Franklin Pierce, had also fought in the Mexican War. Whigs mockingly nicknamed him the Fainting General because he once fainted during battle and had to be carried from the field. The Whigs suggested that Pierce fainted from cowardice, ignoring the fact that his leg was severely injured. They published a one-inch-high book titled *The Military Services of General Pierce*. A ditty about the incident included the verse: "'Tis said that when in Mexico, / While leading on his force, / He took a sudden fainting fit, / And tumbled off his horse." The Whigs also noted that Pierce had a drinking problem, calling him "the hero of many a well-fought bottle."

Pierce beat Scott in a landslide, with 254 electoral votes to Scott's 42. Part of Scott's problem was that the Whigs were deeply divided over the spread of slavery. Southern Whigs either shifted to Pierce, who seemed more supportive of the Compromise of 1850 than Scott, or convened their own mini-conventions and chose alternative candidates. Northern Whigs, angry that the Compromise was part of the party's platform, either stayed away from the polls or voted with antislavery parties like Free Soil.

Scott's humiliating loss was a death blow for the Whig Party. By the next election, most Southern Whigs had fled to the Democrats, while Northern Whigs helped found the new Republican Party.

The Benedict Arnold of 1854

Four years after the Compromise of 1850, the simmering issue of slavery in the territories once again heated up. The crisis arose when Congress proposed establishing a territorial government in the Nebraska Territory. This vast area, part of the Louisiana Purchase, lay north of the 36th parallel, which meant that slavery was illegal there according to the terms of the Missouri Compromise.

Southern congressmen were reluctant to accept such a large free territory into the Union. They feared it would upset the existing balance of power between Free States and slave states.

To resolve this problem, Illinois senator Stephen Douglas proposed the Kansas-Nebraska Act. This legislation repealed the Missouri Compromise and divided the Nebraska Territory in two. Each section would have the right to vote on its own status as slave or free. Northerners felt betrayed by what they called "the Nebraska swindle." Because Douglas's middle name was Arnold, he was labeled the Benedict Arnold of 1854. The *Milwaukee Daily Free Democrat* for April 1, 1854, reports, "Nebraska Douglas was found hung in effigy, from a tree in the Capitol Square, . . . with the following motto: 'Stephen A. Douglas, the Arnold of '54.'"

A group of Ohio women considered Douglas more of a Judas than an Arnold. They sent him thirty pieces of silver. Douglas later commented on the aftermath of the Kansas-Nebraska Act, "I could then travel from Boston to Chicago by the light of my own effigies."

Douglas may have hoped the act would settle territorial slavery issues. Instead, it had the effect of galvanizing partisans on both sides. It also had personal consequences for Douglas. When he ran for reelection to the Senate in 1858, he received an unexpected challenge from Republican Abraham Lincoln. Lincoln had retired from politics after serving briefly in the state legislature and in Congress, but rejoined the fray after the act passed. Although Douglas defeated Lincoln for the Senate, he would have to face him again in 1860.

Bleeding Sumner

Shortly after the Kansas-Nebraska Act passed, Northern abolitionists organized Emigrant Aid Societies to send antislavery settlers to Kansas, with the idea that they would vote to make Kansas a Free State. (For various reasons, everyone assumed Nebraska would be free.) Thousands volunteered to go. At the same time, proslavery Missourians known as Border Ruffians swarmed across the Missouri-Kansas border to stake their own claims. Political hostilities soon escalated into bloody violence, with deaths on both sides. Newspapers named the territory Bleeding Kansas.

On May 19, 1856, Senator Charles Sumner of Massachusetts gave a speech in the Senate titled "The Crime Against Kansas." Using lurid language, he singled out Stephen Douglas and South Carolina senator Andrew Butler as two men who had "raised themselves to eminence . . . in championship of human wrong." Butler, he said, "believes himself a chivalrous knight" whose lady, Slavery, "though ugly to others is always lovely to him."

A few days later, as Sumner was sitting at his desk in the Senate chamber, Butler's nephew, Congressman Preston Brooks, walked up to him. Crying that Sumner's speech was "a libel on South Carolina and on Mr. Butler, who is a relative of mine," he began to beat Sumner over the head with a heavy cane. Sumner, his legs pinned under the desk, was unable to escape the blows. Brooks beat him almost to death before being stopped by two bystanders.

To Northerners, this incident highlighted all the barbarism of the proslavery forces. The badly injured Sumner was revered as a martyr. Republicans attracted hundreds of new followers with the rallying cry "Bleeding Kansas and Bleeding Sumner." Southerners saved their praise for Brooks. He resigned from the House, only to be promptly reelected by his admiring constituents. He received dozens of new canes inscribed with "Hit him again." Bleeding Kansas and Bleeding Sumner destroyed the last hopes that the slavery question could be settled without violence.

1856

James Buchanan (Democrat) vs. John C. Frémont (Republican) vs. Millard Fillmore (Native American)

Miss Nancy's Lockjaw Campaign

For the 1856 election both parties sought candidates who were not too closely associated with any position on the Kansas-Nebraska controversy. The Democratic Party selected James Buchanan, a former senator from Pennsylvania. Buchanan had served as ambassador to England during the passage of the Kansas-Nebraska Act, so had not been forced to take sides.

In fact, Buchanan was a doughface who sympathized with the South, but this attitude would not appear until after the election. Buchanan took the traditionally safe route of not campaigning. He kept such a low profile that Thaddeus Stevens, a fellow Pennsylvanian who supported the Republicans, remarked cuttingly, "There is no such person running as James Buchanan. He is dead of lockjaw. Nothing remains but a platform and a bloated mass of political putridity." Others began referring to Buchanan's strategy as "the lockjaw campaign."

Buchanan's enemies held him in contempt as an ineffectual sissy. He never married, although he had once been briefly engaged. While in Washington, DC, he roomed for fifteen years with Alabama senator William Rufus King. The two were inseparable, giving rise to the rumor that their relationship went beyond simple friendship. One fellow Democrat referred to them as "Buchanan and his wife." Andrew Jackson, who loathed Buchanan, called him "Miss Nancy." The terms *nancy*, *Miss Nancy*, and *Aunt Nancy* first became popular in the early nineteenth century as ways to refer to homosexual or effeminate men.

Questions about Buchanan's sexual inclinations, although the subject of gossip in insider circles, could not be turned into a campaign issue. They remained at the level of whispered rumors. Instead, the Republicans focused on Bleeding Kansas and Bleeding Sumner. They flooded key states with pamphlets decrying slavery and warning white working-class voters about the threat to their jobs if slave labor spread to the territories. The two parties together spent nearly $1 million—an unprecedented amount for political campaigns. Both parties focused on Northern swing states such as Pennsylvania. The South was expected to go solidly for Buchanan.

Buchanan won the election, mainly because many Northern voters still considered Southern secession a greater evil than slavery. He went on to become one of the least effective presidents ever. In modern times he consistently makes ten-worst lists.

Buchanan's troubles included an economic downturn and a mishandled conflict with Utah's Latter-Day Saints (Mormons) known as Buchanan's Blunder. Most serious, when the South seceded after Lincoln's election, Buchanan dithered. During his year-end address to Congress he told Southerners that they had no constitutional right to secede. On the other hand, he said, neither he nor Congress could do anything about it because secession wasn't illegal. Because of his pro-Southern feelings he refused to secure federal forts in the South or call up the militias. His failure to take any positive stand earned him the nickname Old Obliquity.

The Romish Intrigue

Buchanan also won because a third party called the Know-Nothing Party portrayed the Republican candidate, former army officer John C. Frémont, as a secret Catholic. The Know-Nothings, more formally known as the Native American Party, organized in 1843 in response to the perceived double threat of cheap labor and "popery" from the recent influx of European immigrants. Frémont was an Episcopalian, but when he and his wife eloped, they were married by a Catholic priest. The Know-Nothings seized on this fact for their attack. They produced pamphlets with titles like "The Romish Intrigue," "Colonel Frémont's Romanism Established," and "Frémont a Catholic!!"

The Know-Nothings also played on fears that Frémont's election would mean the end of the Union. Their candidate, former president Millard Fillmore, delivered a campaign speech attacking the Republicans for running presidential and vice presidential candidates who were both from Free States. (Frémont was from California, and his running mate was from New Jersey.) Fillmore called this step "moral treason," asking, "Can they have the madness or the folly to imagine that our Southern brethren would submit to be governed by such a Chief Magistrate?"

The South made it clear that they would not tolerate a Republican president. Frémont himself had never expressed radical views about slavery, but the Republican slogan was "Free Labor, Free Speech, Free Men, Free Kansas, Frémont." Southern Democrats retorted with the ugly parody, "Free Soilers, Frémonters, free niggers and free booters." Southern newspapers reported that plans were moving forward for immediate secession if the election didn't go the right way.

This threat had its effect. Buchanan not only carried the South, but Pennsylvania, New Jersey, Indiana, Illinois, and California. Although Maryland was the only state to go for Fillmore, he won 21 percent of the popular vote. Frémont joined the list of presidential candidates ambushed by a third party and the South remained in the Union another four years.

The 1856 election was the high point for the Know-Nothings. Afterward, they quickly declined, and by 1860 had disappeared.

Jayhawkers and Bushwhackers

Jayhawker was a name first given to antislavery raiders in Bleeding Kansas. James Montgomery and his band may have inspired the term. Montgomery was a committed abolitionist who harried proslavery Kansans before the Civil War. According to one writer of the period, the name was "universally applied to Montgomery's men, from the celerity of their movements and their habit of suddenly pouncing upon an enemy." When the war began, Montgomery was made a colonel in the Union Army. He and his men conducted frequent Jayhawker-style raids into Missouri. During and after the war, the term broadened to mean any guerrilla soldier operating in Kansas, then any sort of plunderer. Jayhawkers and other guerrillas often pillaged the area during their raids.

Bushwhackers could be on either side, although the term applied more often to Southerners. In the early United States, the word simply meant a backwoods dweller—someone who had to whack through the bush. The 1809 *Knickerbocker's History of New York* describes an early New York family as "gallant bush-whackers and hunters of raccoons by moon-light."

During the Kansas conflict and the Civil War, *Bushwhacker* was a term for backwoods fighters conducting guerrilla warfare. As with *Jayhawker*, the word implied a looter. It also developed the figurative meaning of an underhanded attack. A February 1845 *Congressional Globe* reports, "All [Senator Foster of Tennessee] asked for was a clear field and a fair fight—no bush-whacking."

1860

ABRAHAM LINCOLN (REPUBLICAN) VS. STEPHEN DOUGLAS (DEMOCRAT) VS. JOHN BRECKINRIDGE (DEMOCRAT) VS. JOHN BELL (CONSTITUTIONAL UNION)

Rail Splitter

The Republicans' nomination of Abraham Lincoln for the presidency came as an unwelcome surprise to many people. He was not prominent in politics, having served only a few terms in the Illinois legislature and one term in Congress. He had run twice for the Senate and lost. Democratic newspapers expressed their astonishment that this "slang-whanging stump speaker" had been chosen over more accomplished men. In an editorial written shortly after the nomination, the *New York Herald* described Lincoln as a "third-rate western lawyer" and "a fourth-rate lecturer who cannot speak good grammar." The paper reminded readers that Lincoln had recently been in New York, delivering a lecture of "unmitigated trash, interlarded with coarse and clumsy jokes" and filling his pockets "with dollars coined out of republican fanaticism."

The two main sources of ridicule were Lincoln's lowly origins and his homely looks. Said the *Rochester Advertiser*, "He is a man of few talents, a self-made man, a tall, swarthy, rather cadaverous-looking Kentuckian." The *Philadelphia Evening Journal* complained of his "coarse language" and "illiterate style." "It does not by any means follow," said the paper, "that because an individual . . . beginning life as a flat-boatman and wood-chopper, raises himself to the position of . . . County Court Lawyer . . . [he] is therefore qualified to be President." The *Houston Telegraph* called Lincoln "the leanest, lankest, most ungainly mass of legs and arms and hatchet face that was ever strung on a single frame."

Both sides made much of Lincoln's early history as a backwoods "rail splitter." One Democratic paper made up a story describing how, when the nominating committee came to tell Lincoln he was the Republican choice, they found him out in his woods splitting rails. In the punch line of the story, he tells the committee not to pester him: "I've only got two hundred thousand rails to split before sundown. I kin do it if you'll let me alone." Democrats campaigned with the slogan "We want a statesman, not a rail splitter, for president."

Republicans retorted that Lincoln had split rails but his opponent Stephen Douglas split the Democratic Party. They said that Douglas was a rail spelled backward—a liar. At the Republican convention, the Ohio delegate Columbus Delano nominated Lincoln with the words, "I rise . . . to put in nomination a man who can split rails and maul Democrats—Abraham Lincoln."

Douglas was called the Steam Engine in Britches because of his tireless campaigning. Open stumping was still not completely acceptable, so he let it be known that he was traveling to visit his mother in New York—with stops along the way. This story induced hilarity in the Republicans, who printed broadsides headed, "Boy Lost!" Underneath, they said, "Left Washington, DC, some time in July. . . . He has not yet reached his mother, who is very anxious about him." The posters further described him as "about five feet nothing in height and about the same in diameter the other way . . . talks a great deal, very loud, always about himself."

Lincoln won the presidency not because voters overwhelmingly wanted him but because the rift between Northern and Southern Democrats had widened beyond repair. When Douglas refused to accept a platform guaranteeing that slavery would be legal in the territories, Southern Democrats walked out of the convention. They nominated their own candidate, John Breckinridge of Kentucky. The few remaining Whigs gathered under the banner of the Constitutional Union Party (known humorously as the Do-Nothings because of their lack of platform) to nominate John Bell of Tennessee.

With one of the largest voter turnouts in American history— over 80 percent—Lincoln won every Northern state except New Jersey. Although the other three candidates together won more total votes than he did, he won a plurality of the popular vote and a large majority of the electoral vote. As soon as Lincoln's win became known, the South began preparing for secession. By December, South Carolina had left the Union. Other Southern states soon followed, and by April, the country was at war.

Cotton Whigs, Butternuts, and Copperheads

Political positions before and during the Civil War were not always predictable. In Northern states such as Massachusetts, where the economy depended on keeping the cotton mills running, some Whigs were ready to accept the continued spread of slavery. Called Cotton Whigs, they feared that slavery's curtailment would raise the price of cotton. Their antislavery opponents were called Conscience Whigs. Conscience Whigs were also negatively referred to as Woolly Heads or, after the founding of the Republican Party, Black Republicans. Conscience Whigs sometimes called the Cotton Whigs the Silver Grays because most were old enough to have hair that color. They were considered the old fogies' wing of the party.

Even during the war, some Northerners did not support the Union cause. Those who sympathized with the South were called Butternuts. The bark of the butternut tree was used to dye homespun fabric a brownish gray. Confederate uniforms were often described as "butternut colored," although most weren't actually dyed with butternut bark. Hard-line abolitionists during the war called all Democrats Butternuts.

As the years passed with few Union victories, increasing numbers of Northerners became disenchanted with the fight. Those who wanted an immediate end to the war and recognition of the Confederacy called themselves Peace Democrats. Their opponents labeled them Copperheads. The name came from the poisonous snake common throughout most of the South.

Political Copperheads were especially numerous in areas bordering the Confederacy, such as the southern parts of Illinois, Indiana, and Ohio. Many of the people living in these regions were originally from the South or had relatives there. Large numbers of recent German and Irish immigrants also rallied around Copperhead principles. Racism played a large part in their attitudes. Many people feared social upheaval if the slaves were freed. Some also worried about the resulting competition for jobs.

Copperheads also resented the draft. They were especially angry over a provision that allowed draftees to hire a substitute or buy their way out with a payment of $300. That amount of money represented almost a year's wages for a working-class man. Although in theory the draft applied equally to all male citizens, in practice the wealthy and well connected could avoid service if they wanted to. The Democrats fanned the flames of Copperhead discontent with slogans such as "Three Hundred Dollars or Your Life."

As so often happened during this era, hostile rhetoric escalated into violence. On July 13, 1863, New York City exploded in four days of rioting, looting, and destruction later known as the Draft

Riots. The violence claimed the lives of more than a hundred people, many of them black men lynched by the mob. Army units had to be recalled from Gettysburg to bring the city under control.

In late 1862 opponents of the war started wearing Copperhead Badges, also called Badges of Liberty. These were made by taking old-style large copper pennies, featuring Lady Liberty's profile, and cutting away all but the head. Tokens were also created that resembled these reshaped pennies. The first Copperhead Badges are thought to have been made in Cincinnati, Ohio.

Mossbacks

Many Southern men avoided the draft by hiding in swamps or backwoods. They were known as Mossbacks because they supposedly stayed crouched out in the swamps for so long that moss had time to grow on their backs. The term may have originated in North Carolina, where poor swamp dwellers before the war were also called Mossbacks.

Figuratively speaking, a Mossback was someone who hunkered down in an established position and stayed there. In post–Civil War Ohio, the Democratic Party's conservative wing was briefly known as the Mossback Party.

In recent decades people have used the term *mossback* to refer to a reactionary generally, but especially in politics. A good example comes from *Newsweek* for December 23, 1991: "With party mossbacks on one side and radical reformers on the other."

1864

ABRAHAM LINCOLN (NATIONAL UNION/ REPUBLICAN) VS. GEORGE MCCLELLAN (DEMOCRAT)

Ignoramus Abe

Copperhead newspapers attacked Abraham Lincoln ceaselessly throughout his time in office. This verbal abuse reached a peak in 1864, as the country faced the challenge of a presidential election during wartime. Anti-Lincoln newspapers still frequently portrayed the president as an ignorant hick. After Lincoln and Tennessean Andrew Johnson received the Republican nomination, the *New York World* fulminated: "The age of statesmen is gone; the age of rail splitters . . . has succeeded. . . . In a crisis of the most appalling magnitude . . . the country is asked to consider the claims of two ignorant, boorish, third-rate backwoods lawyers." Ignoramus Abe was one of the nicknames flung at him. Others, as recorded by *Harper's Weekly* for September 24, 1864, included *Despot, Liar, Thief, Buffoon,* and *Old Scoundrel.*

Not only the press, but the public held Lincoln to blame for the military disasters of the past three years. Even many loyal Republicans questioned whether he should run again. The Radical Republican wing of the party also felt that he had not gone far enough to abolish slavery, and they feared that he would be too conciliatory toward the South after the war. They chose to run Frémont as an alternative candidate. Lincoln and Johnson ran on the National Union Party ticket.

Northern Democrats nominated General George McClellan, whom Lincoln had recently relieved from command of the Union Army. Their slogan was, "Old Abe removed McClellan. We'll now remove Old Abe." The Democrats published a forty-six-page pamphlet titled "The Lincoln Catechism" that used a question-and-answer format to attack the president. Questions ranged from "What was Abraham Lincoln by trade? A rail-splitter. What is he now? A union splitter." to "Should Mr. Lincoln be re-elected, what debt will he leave upon the country at the end of his second term? Eight billions, or *eight thousand millions*, of dollars!"

Republicans responded with "The Copperhead Catechism." It begins with the question, "What is the chief aim of a Copperhead in this life? The chief aim of a Copperhead is to abuse the President, vilify the Administration, and glorify himself before the people."

Lincoln himself did not expect to win a second term. However, shortly before the election General Sherman captured Atlanta and the tide of the war shifted. Republican morale began to rise. Frémont eventually withdrew his candidacy and Republicans united behind Lincoln. In the end Lincoln won a sweeping victory over McClellan, taking every state except Kentucky, Delaware, and New Jersey.

Mudslingers and Soreheads

In the mid-nineteenth century, *mudslinger* became the label of choice for politicians who resort to insults and slander to bring down their opponents. For instance, Indiana's *Logansport Weekly Journal* for December 18, 1875, after refuting charges of Republican hanky-panky during a military trial, snaps, "Hunt up another object of abuse, Democratic mudslingers." *Mudslinging campaign* was being flung around freely by the early twentieth century.

Soreheads—dissatisfied politicians—were also on the rise in the late nineteenth century. An article in an 1878 issue of *North American Review* describes the 1872 convention of breakaway Liberal Republicans this way: "renegade Republicans . . . all shouting for reform; all vociferating against Republican rascality; each led by a little faction of soreheads, desperate and reckless." The word may have derived from the expression *like a bear with a sore head* to describe someone in an extremely crabby mood.

The expression *like a bear with a sore head*, probably the inspiration for *sorehead*, is no longer heard in the United States. However, it is still familiar in England and Australia. In the twentieth century, *sorehead* has lost its political connotations and can apply to any disgruntled person.

Lame Ducks

In the early nineteenth century, lame ducks were speculators on the stock exchange who couldn't meet their debts. More generally, the term could mean any weak or incapacitated person. That usage no doubt explains how *lame duck* expanded to cover a politician who either had not been reelected or was not likely to be. In one of the earliest uses in print, the *Congressional Globe* for January 1863 defines lame ducks as "broken down politicians."

Until 1933 new administrations did not take office until March.

This gap allowed plenty of time for election results to be counted and for new officeholders to travel to Washington. Between the election and the changeover, Congress held a short session that inevitably included a number of legislators known to be on their way out. By the 1860s, this was called the lame duck session.

In 1932, the Twentieth Amendment, known as the "Lame Duck" Amendment, abolished this gap session. The new congressional term now starts at noon on January 3, and the president's and vice president's terms at noon on January 20. Modern lame ducks are politicians who can't legally run for office again or who have announced that they're stepping down.

1868

ULYSSES GRANT (REPUBLICAN) VS. HORATIO SEYMOUR (DEMOCRAT)

Grant the Butcher

The 1868 presidential election was mainly about the Civil War. Although hostilities had ended three years earlier, feelings on both sides were still running high. The political parties reflected the sharp sectional differences that continued to divide the country. Republicans, "the party of Lincoln," ran a Union war hero for president. Democrats, the party of the "solid South," ran a Copperhead.

While General Ulysses S. Grant was an easy choice for Republicans, the Democrats struggled through more than twenty ballots before settling on a dark horse candidate, former New

York governor Horatio Seymour. Seymour was flustered by the unexpected nomination. At first he declared that he could not be a candidate. Then he became weepy and was led off the platform by his friends. Although he accepted the nomination immediately afterward, Republicans leaped gleefully on this sign of weakness, labeling Seymour the Great Decliner.

If Seymour was surprised by the nomination, others were stunned. As a Peace Democrat during the war, Seymour had held opinions that many in the Union considered traitorous. Republican newspapers hit this note hard. They reminded voters that then-Governor Seymour had addressed the New York draft rioters with the unfortunate phrase, "My friends." The *New York Herald* called Seymour "the embodiment of Copperheadism." The *New York Tribune* declared that if Seymour could be elected over Grant, "the patriot blood poured out like water at Gettysburg, Vicksburg, Mission Ridge and in the advance to Richmond was shed in vain." The paper told its readers, "Scratch a Democrat and you'll find a Rebel under his skin."

Seymour lived up to this reputation by running a racist campaign, accusing Grant and the Republicans of wanting to "Africanize" the South. Democrats were bitter that the army had been sent into several Southern states to enforce Reconstruction. They portrayed Grant as a would-be military dictator—"the man on horseback"—and sneered at his campaign slogan, "Let us have peace." The Democratic vice presidential candidate Francis Blair wrote, "The peace to which Grant invites us is the peace of despotism and death."

Grant may have been a hero to most Northerners, but to his

critics he was Grant the Butcher. They reminded voters that his battles against the Confederate Army in northern Virginia had been the bloodiest of the war. He had won, but at a terrible cost. Grant had also gained a wartime reputation as a serious alcoholic. The Democrats claimed he had been seen "drunk in the public streets" even after his nomination. Anti-Grant parades featured placards with the slogans "Grant the Butcher," "Grant the Drunkard," and "Grant talks peace but makes war."

Republicans responded with "Grant acts, Seymour talks, Blair blows." They said that Blair was as much a drunkard as anybody, pointing to a two-day hotel bill that listed $10 for room and board and $60 for whiskey and lemons. As for Seymour, they hinted that there was insanity in the family.

Grant refused to campaign, which led the Democrats to call him "the deaf and dumb candidate." However, as Election Day drew near, it became clear that Grant's status as a war hero was enough to make him popular with voters. The Democrats began to fear a landslide defeat. One faction of the party clamored for Seymour to step down in favor of Chief Justice Salmon Chase. Seymour embarked on a frantic last-minute speaking tour to build support, but to no avail. He carried only eight states.

Although Grant won by a wide margin of electoral votes, his share of the popular vote was much narrower. He probably could not have achieved a popular majority without the votes of black men who went to the polls for the first time in 1868—another reflection of the Civil War's political impact.

★ 3 ★

Carpetbaggers and Boodlers

RECONSTRUCTION AND THE GILDED AGE

1872–1896

After the Civil War, the country remained as divided as ever. The dominant Republican Party struggled over how to handle Reconstruction. They pushed through the Fourteenth and Fifteenth Amendments, giving African Americans citizenship and black men the right to vote, but they had to send troops into southern states to enforce the new laws.

Graft, corruption, and fraud thrived in the postwar chaos. Enterprising northerners traveled south to take advantage of any pickings on offer, and many southerners were equally willing to exploit the disaster. Politicians at all levels took their cue from the Grant administration, where wide-scale corruption flourished. The late nineteenth century is one of the few eras to be known by a negative nickname—the Gilded Age, from the title of Mark Twain's 1873 novel portraying unabashed greed and political opportunism.

As Reconstruction ended and wartime issues faded, personal attacks once again gained favor as a campaign tactic. The candidates' private lives, intellects, religious beliefs, and appearance remained rich sources of ammunition for their opponents. One appalled observer called the 1884 presidential contest between Grover Cleveland and James G. Blaine "the vilest ever waged."

Waving the Bloody Shirt

Republicans never lost an opportunity to remind voters that pro-southern Democrats were responsible for the Civil War. When other issues failed, they could always stir up the crowd with emotional references to Gettysburg, Vicksburg, and "patriot blood." Southerners, resentful of these reminders, began calling this tactic *waving the bloody shirt.* The phrase alludes to a speech in the House of Representatives that allegedly featured the bloody shirt of a Ku Klux Klan victim.

Although the newly formed Ku Klux Klan concentrated on terrorizing African Americans, they sometimes went after white Reconstructionists as well. In the "bloody shirt" incident, the Klan appeared late at night at the home of a former Ohioan named A. P. Huggins, now a school superintendent and tax collector in Mississippi. They roused him out of bed, told him to clear out of town, and then gave him seventy-five lashes with a leather strap.

Huggins reported the incident to the military. Afterward, one of the officers carried Huggins's bloodstained nightshirt to Representative Benjamin F. Butler, Radical Republican of Massachusetts. During an impassioned speech demanding stronger action against the Klan, Butler supposedly waved the shirt around as a prop.

Representative Butler definitely gave an impassioned speech, but the detail of his waving the bloody shirt was probably an embellishment. Reports of the occasion don't mention it. Whether literal or figurative, the expression caught on. It was especially popular with the Democratic newspapers. One example comes from the *Placerville (CA) Mountain Democrat* for October 28, 1876: "Republican leaders . . . wave the bloody shirt [and] appeal to sectional hatred."

The Republican Party waved the bloody shirt with great success until 1884. That's when Grover Cleveland became the first Democrat elected to the White House since James Buchanan—a gap of twenty-eight years.

The expression *wave the bloody shirt* is still popular among political commentators, although the incident originally referred to has long been forgotten. The term has now broadened to mean any kind of inflammatory political rhetoric.

Carpetbaggers and Scalawags

As the federal government started the process of Reconstruction, many northerners headed south. Some were there to help—as schoolmasters, public officials, and the like. Others were opportunists, looking to exploit the South's troubles for profit. They arrived with their belongings packed in carpetbags, soft-sided traveling bags upholstered in carpet. Before the war, the term *carpetbagger* referred to a "wildcat" banker in the West—that is, a banker with no fixed address, who made loans from the money he carried in his bag.

After 1865 the word designated northerners working in the postwar South. The military governments established in the South during Reconstruction became known as carpetbag governments. By the 1870s, *carpetbagger* was a contemptuous term for any transient or stranger, wherever he was from.

Scalawags were the southern counterparts of carpetbaggers. They saw Reconstruction as a chance to get their hands on some government cash. The two words were often paired, as in this line from the July 18, 1868, *New York Herald*: "There was nothing left in his old State but scallawags and carpet baggers." Before the war, *scalawag* simply meant "a rascal." Westerners also called scrawny cattle *scalawags*, and this use might have been the original one.

Grantism

As the 1872 election drew near, Grant's administration was beset by scandal. Historians agree that Grant himself was honest, but he was easily manipulated by smooth talkers who gave him valuable presents. He often rewarded them with government appointments. The so-called spoils system—the tradition of officeholders handing out plum Civil Service jobs to relatives and friends—went back to the days of Andrew Jackson. However, it reached new levels during the post–Civil War period.

The entire administration was riddled with fraud and corruption. Even when confronted with evidence that his appointees were crooked, Grant was reluctant to fire them. Several bribery and embezzlement scandals came to light during Grant's tenure, inspiring newspapers to coin a new term for brazen dishonesty in government—*Grantism*.

One high-profile scheme was known as the Crédit Mobilier scandal. This fraud involved the Union Pacific Railroad Company creating a dummy construction company, Crédit Mobilier, to build its government-funded railroad line. Crédit Mobilier billed Union Pacific (that is, itself) at an inflated rate. Union Pacific then added a hefty handling charge and passed along the final bill to the government. To ensure that no inconvenient questions were asked, the directors sold shares of stock to congressmen at below-market prices. Eventually the newspapers got wind of the scheme, provoking an investigation that implicated over two dozen officeholders of both parties.

The Whiskey Ring scandal was not exposed until Grant's second term. This complicated system of bribery and kickbacks originated with the Republican Party in St. Louis but spread to other major cities. Tax collectors and whiskey distillers skimmed off millions of federal tax dollars before the treasury secretary exposed the ring. More than two hundred people were indicted, including President Grant's private secretary.

Iowa's *Jackson Sentinel* expressed the mood of the country in 1875 when it said, "The people are weary to loathing of Grantism." Disgust with the systemic corruption led to mounting calls for Civil Service reform. It also helped bring an end to Reconstruction, now connected in the public mind with a discredited administration.

1872

Ulysses Grant (Republican) vs. Horace Greeley (Radical Republican/Democrat)

Old White Hat

Part of the reason Grant was reelected in 1872 is that the full scope of his administration's corruption was unknown at the time of the election. Another reason is that an unlikely coalition of Radical Republicans and Democrats ran one of the worst candidates they could have chosen—Horace Greeley, longtime crusading editor of the *New York Tribune*. (Greeley is now best known for the editorial advice "Go west, young man.")

Impatient with continued government corruption, Radical

Republicans held a splinter nominating convention in Cincinnati. They chose Horace Greeley as their alternative to Grant. Greeley was politically influential through his newspaper. He was also unquestionably honest. On the negative side, he was highly eccentric—a vegetarian teetotaler who espoused various fringe causes, including Fourierism, a system for reorganizing society into self-sustaining cooperatives. Greeley was also eccentric-looking. Potbellied, bald, and with scruffy whiskers, he wore a white hat and duster in every kind of weather.

Greeley would have remained a minor candidate except that the Democrats—with no obvious choices of their own and eager to run someone dramatically different from Grant—accepted Greeley as the Democratic candidate also. In modern terms, this situation is similar to the Socialist Workers Party nominating a candidate and the Republicans deciding to run the same person. After the Cincinnati convention, one astounded observer wrote to a friend, "I did not suppose that any considerable number of men, outside of a Lunatic Asylum, would nominate Greeley for President." Now two parties had chosen him.

Greeley was a gift for Grant supporters. He was widely known as Old White Hat because of his invariable headgear, but his Republican opponents called him several other names as well. He was Old Bailbonds because he had provided part of Jefferson Davis's bail after the war; Old Four Hundred Millions because he had suggested to Lincoln that the government buy the South's slaves for that sum; Old Let 'Em Go because in 1864 he pushed to negotiate with the Confederacy; and Old Villain-You-Lie because he often used that phrase.

In a brutal editorial of August 3, 1872, *Harper's Weekly* points out the absurdity of Greeley, a Radical Republican, running as a Democrat. The editor notes that most of the positions Greeley has taken in the past directly oppose what the Democrats stand for. He ends the piece by quoting Greeley's own words before his nomination, when speculating about a Democratic success in 1872: "Whatever chastisement may be deserved by our national sins, we must hope that this disgrace and humiliation may be spared us." The *Harper's* editor heartily concurs.

Of course Greeley never had a chance. He won only 63 electoral votes out of 349. He commented ruefully, "I was the worst beaten man who ever ran for high office." Greeley's life came to a melancholy end shortly after the election. He sank into a state of mental confusion, perhaps triggered by his wife's recent death. He began hallucinating and was taken to a mental institution, where he died a few weeks later.

Pork-Barrel Spending

During this period of rampant government fraud, cutting a juicy deal was described as going to the pork barrel. Real pork barrels—thirty-one-gallon barrels holding salted pork—were a common feature of nineteenth-century households. Americans ate a lot of pork, the cheapest meat to raise. A full pork barrel at the start of winter meant protection against hunger. Likewise, congressmen and civil servants during the Grant administrations provided for the future by helping themselves to available government funds.

One of the first figurative uses of *pork barrel* appears in the *Defi-*

ance Democrat for September 13, 1873. Writing about the furor over a recent legislative pay raise, the paper says, "A good many honorable Senators and Representatives . . . are scared but they are also aggrieved. . . . Recollecting their many previous visits to the public pork-barrel . . . [and] the utter indifference displayed by the people, this hue-and-cry over the salary grab . . . puzzles quite as much as it alarms them." *Pork-barrel spending* gradually came to mean designating money for local projects that would please constituents.

1876

RUTHERFORD HAYES (REPUBLICAN) VS. SAMUEL TILDEN (DEMOCRAT)

Ruther-fraud Beats Slippery Sam

The great irony of the 1876 presidential election was that both major candidates were known as reformers. Yet the election was one of the most crooked in American history. The Republicans, weary of the disasters of Grantism, nominated Ohio governor Rutherford B. Hayes, respected for his honesty. Democrats chose Samuel J. Tilden, New York's crusading governor. Tilden had smashed the Tweed Ring, a group of embezzling politicians led by Tammany Hall's "Boss" Tweed. Both men supported Civil Service reform, the removal of corrupt officeholders, and an end to Reconstruction.

With no sharp political differences between the candidates,

both campaigns resorted to mudslinging. The Democrats had plenty of material—the malfeasance of Grant appointees, the failures of Reconstruction, the ongoing economic slump. It was difficult to find mud to throw at Hayes himself, a staid family man, but the Democrats managed a couple of smears. They put a negative spin on an incident during the war when Hayes "stole" money from a deserter about to be executed. (He actually sent the money to the man's family.) They also said he had once gotten drunk and accidentally shot his mother in the arm, a story later proved false.

The Republicans responded by vigorously waving the bloody shirt. In a widely quoted speech given before a group of Indianapolis veterans, famed orator Robert Ingersoll reminded his audience, "Every man that shot Union soldiers was a Democrat. . . . Every man that loved slavery better than liberty was a Democrat. . . . The man that assassinated Abraham Lincoln was a Democrat." Republicans also attacked Tilden personally. They accused him of tax evasion, of being sympathetic toward slavery, of getting rich as a lawyer who defended corporate criminals. They called him Soapy Sam and Slippery Sam. They even accused him—wrongly—of having syphilis, which they claimed had affected his brain.

Nor did the dirty tricks stop at name calling. The Republicans tried to bully African Americans into voting their way—more than once where possible—and the Democrats tried to terrorize them into not voting at all. Ballot-box stuffing was rampant on both sides. Reportedly, in some districts party bosses stood by the ballot boxes and openly tore up any votes handed in for the "wrong" candidate.

The earliest election results indicated that Tilden had won. He had 184 electoral votes, only one short of what he needed. The returns were still out for Louisiana, South Carolina, and Florida. These happened to be the three remaining carpetbag states, with governments under Republican control. Seeing an opportunity, Republican committee chairman Zachariah Chandler telegraphed to Republican election officials in those states, saying, "Hayes is elected if we have carried South Carolina, Florida, and Louisiana. Can you hold your state?"

As a result, all three states returned competing sets of electoral votes—a Democratic set in favor of Tilden and a Republican set in favor of Hayes. A disputed electoral vote in Oregon, eventually awarded to Hayes, further muddied the waters.

Both parties sent officials south to investigate voting irregularities. Then began a period of intense wrangling that ended when Congress appointed a fifteen-man commission to decide the matter—seven Republicans, seven Democrats, and one Independent. At the last minute, the Independent was elected to the Senate and resigned from the commission. A Republican took his place, with predictable results. On March 2, 1877, the commission decided 8–7 in favor of Hayes.

The Democrats took their defeat badly. Southern hotheads organized under the banner "Tilden or blood." While Hayes was at dinner with his family one evening, someone fired a bullet through his parlor window, fortunately not hitting anyone. Meanwhile, behind the scenes, the Hayes people were negotiating. Hayes agreed to remove the last troops from the carpetbag states if they would accept the Republican version of the election results. He also agreed to name a southerner to his cabinet.

Tilden withdrew his claim to the presidency, although he always believed that he was the genuine winner. He won the majority of the popular vote, and some historians believe that in a fair election, he would have carried Louisiana and Florida. He later told his campaign manager that he preferred four years of the Hayes administration to four years of civil war. Other Democrats were less reconciled. They called President Hayes His Fraudulency, Ruther-fraud, or Old Eight to Seven.

Amen Corner

The amen corner was originally the spot in a church reserved for worshipers who liked to participate actively in the service by shouting "Amen!" at regular intervals. In the late nineteenth century, it also referred to the gathering place of political yes-men.

The first political amen corner was located in the lobby of New York City's Fifth Avenue Hotel, a popular Republican meeting spot from the 1860s onward. When New York senator Thomas C. Platt lived there, party bigwigs used to visit him on Sunday mornings to plot strategy. Small-fry were not invited, so they congregated in the lobby. One morning a reporter walked by and asked them what they were doing there. Someone explained that the "big chiefs" were upstairs conferring, while their followers waited in the lobby to "say 'amen'" to whatever those at the meeting decided.

In the 1880s the area of the Senate where party stalwarts sat also began to be called the amen corner. An early example of the nickname's use comes from an 1884 *Congressional Record*: "When commiserated upon the fact that he was compelled to go to what is commonly known here as the amen corner, [the new senator] frankly said that any seat in the Senate was better than none."

1880

JAMES GARFIELD (REPUBLICAN) VS. WINFIELD SCOTT HANCOCK (DEMOCRAT)

Taking a break from the hysteria of 1876 (and perhaps gearing up for the vicious 1884 election), both parties ran uninspired campaigns in 1880. There were no serious disagreements on policy and the mud was recycled.

The Democrats tried to tar Republican candidate James Garfield with the brush of Grantism, claiming that he took a $389 bribe from Crédit Mobilier. Their accusation lost some of its punch when Garfield explained that the money was actually a loan, which he had repaid. The Republicans were even less inspired in their attacks, once again reminding voters that the Democrats were to blame for the Civil War. As Democratic candidate Winfield Scott Hancock had been a much-admired Union general during that war, this accusation also fell a little flat.

Both parties then resorted to the time-honored tactics of vote buying and ballot-box stuffing. The Republicans were slightly more successful in their efforts, giving Garfield an extremely narrow win. Four months later he was assassinated by a rejected office seeker. The vice president, Chester Arthur, served out the remainder of Garfield's term, but did not run for reelection.

1884

GROVER CLEVELAND (DEMOCRAT) VS. JAMES G. BLAINE (REPUBLICAN)

Rum, Romanism, and Rebellion

The 1884 presidential campaign came down to a choice between a candidate with a blameless personal life but a record of shady business dealings and a candidate with a spotless public record but a sordid personal history. The campaign was notable for the amount and type of dirt thrown. However, the worst blow to the loser came from one of his own supporters.

The Republicans nominated James G. Blaine. Although tremendously popular inside the party, Blaine had previously been passed over because of his involvement in questionable business schemes such as the Crédit Mobilier. According to one critic, he had "wallowed in spoils like a rhinoceros in an African pool." This time, his supporters were able to generate enough enthusiasm to sweep him onto the ticket. The Democrats chose New York governor Grover Cleveland, known to his constituents as Grover the Good for his sterling integrity.

Soon after the contest opened, the mud began to fly. The *Boston Journal* published a handful of indiscreet business letters written by Blaine. These included one to railroad attorney Warren

Fisher that ended "Kind regards to Mrs. Fisher. Burn this letter!" The Democrats were delighted—they began chanting, "Kind regards to Mrs. Fisher! Burn this letter!" They called Blaine Slippery Jim and made up the rhyme, "Blaine, Blaine, James G. Blaine, / Continental liar from the state of Maine!"

The worst the Republicans could say of Cleveland was that he was naive and inexperienced in government affairs. They also made fun of his weight—about 250 pounds—by saying that he was "a small man everywhere except on the hay scales." Then the *Buffalo Evening Telegram* broke the sensational story that the unmarried Cleveland had fathered a child out of wedlock.

Under the title "A *Terrible* Tale: A Dark Chapter in a Public Man's History," the paper revealed that when Cleveland was a young Buffalo lawyer, he had an affair with a thirty-six-year-old widow named Maria Halpin and fathered a son by her. Cleveland admitted that he had been involved with Halpin, although the child's paternity was unclear. Some historians have speculated that the boy actually belonged to Cleveland's deceased law partner, Oscar Folsom. However, Cleveland had provided support to both mother and child in the past.

The Republicans made the most of Grover the Good's sex scandal, shouting, "Ma, Ma, where's my Pa?" After the election, victorious Democrats responded with "Gone to the White House, ha ha ha!" More seriously, Republican newspapers questioned whether the American people could elect "a coarse debauchee who would bring his harlots with him to Washington." Rumors circulated that Cleveland was a habitual womanizer. A Buffalo clergyman named George W. Ball wrote to the newspapers, claiming to have evidence of "debaucheries too horrible to relate and too vile to be readily believed." Democrats argued that Cleveland's qualities as a principled politician were more important than his private life.

Over Cleveland's objections, Democrats also spread the story that the Blaines had a shotgun wedding. (They had been married twice because there was some question about the first ceremony's legality. Their first child was born three months after the second wedding.)

With plenty of scandal to go around, the contest was close. Then on one disastrous day, Blaine's campaign derailed. On the morning of "Black Wednesday," October 29, Republicans held a meeting at the Fifth Avenue Hotel. One speaker was Presbyterian minister S. D. Burchard. Burchard wound up his emotional speech by describing the Democrats as "the party of Rum, Romanism, and Rebellion." The first two words were a slam against Irish Catholic immigrants, whom Blaine could not afford to anger if he hoped to carry New York.

Unfortunately, Blaine didn't repudiate Burchard's inflammatory line. He later explained to a friend that he was concentrating on his own upcoming speech and didn't notice what was said. Others did. The next morning the Democratic papers spread news of the slur far and wide. For good measure, the Cleveland campaign printed thousands of leaflets emblazoned with the words "Rum, Romanism, and Rebellion!" and distributed them throughout New York's Irish neighborhoods.

That same evening, unaware of his impending doom, Blaine attended a fund-raising dinner at Delmonico's Restaurant, in company with several millionaires. Those still suffering through the recent depression were not happy to read in the *New York World* the next day about "The Royal Feast of Belshazzar Blaine and the Money Kings," comparing Blaine to the prince of Baby-lon who feasted while the Persians marched toward his city. "From Rum, Romanism, and Rebellion at the Fifth Avenue Hotel," the paper announced, "Mr. Blaine proceeded to the Merry Banquet of the Millionaires at Delmonico's, where champagne frothed and brandy sparkled in glasses that glittered like jewels."

On Election Day, Blaine lost New York by a little over one thousand votes, and hence the election. Cleveland became the first Democratic president since before the Civil War.

Mugwumps

Mugwump comes from an Algonquian word meaning "a war leader." During the nineteenth century, Americans used it hu-morously to refer to a man who was not quite as important or superior as he imagined. The word became a label for the Radical Republicans during the 1884 campaign.

The reforming wing of the Republican Party had been agitat-ing to clean up government since the days of President Grant. Blaine's nomination disgusted them. When Cleveland became the Democratic candidate they announced that they were jump-ing the Republican ship in favor of an honest man.

The party faithful sneered at this holier-than-thou attitude. Republican newspapers began calling the deserters mugwumps, which the *New York Sun* translated freely as "big bug or swell head." Other Republican newspapers called them soreheads, goody-goodies, doctrinaires, holy Willies, bolters, and assistant Democrats. They were also frequently referred to as Half-Breeds, in contrast to loyal Blaine supporters who were known as Stalwarts. In a June 20, 1884, editorial, the *New York Evening Post* remarks, "We have yet to see a Blaine organ which speaks of the Independent Republicans otherwise than as Pharisees, hypocrites, dudes, mugwumps, transcendentalists or something of that sort."

Over time, *mugwump* took on the more general meaning of someone who switches party allegiance whenever it's convenient. This definition probably accounts for the word's folk etymology—a politician whose mug is on one side of the fence while his wump is on the other.

Boodlers and Snollygosters

Words for scoundrels were plentiful during the Gilded Age. Beginning in the 1880s, boodlers were politicians who lined their pockets with profits from bribery, graft, and fraud. Cash that party bosses doled out to reward faithful supporters was also known as boodle.

Boodle is an old word, adopted from New York's early Dutch settlers. Originally it meant someone's estate or possessions. It later evolved into underworld jargon for counterfeit money and finally into slang for ill-gotten gains in general. Such terms as *boodler*, *boodleizing*, *boodle politician*, and the verb *to boodle* were common in nineteenth-century newspaper editorials. For instance, an 1887 *Nation* editorial declares with exasperation, "New York is better known all over the . . . world for boodle Aldermen and municipal rings than for anything else."

By the early twentieth century the word had lost its political meaning. *Boodle* is now close to being obsolete, but is still used occasionally to mean any kind of contraband.

Even less familiar than *boodler* these days is the fantastical coinage *snollygoster*. This word was popularized almost single-handedly by a Georgia Democrat named H. J. W. Ham, who traveled around the country during the 1890s with a stump speech titled "The Snollygoster in Politics." Ham claimed to have first heard the word during an 1848 political debate. He defined a snollygoster as a "place-hunting demagogue" or a "political hypocrite." The *Columbus Dispatch* for October 28, 1895, captures the spirit of the word with this more elaborate definition: "A snollygoster is a fellow who wants office, regardless of party, platform or principles, and who, whenever he wins, gets there by the sheer force of monumental talknophical assumnancy."

It's unclear how *snollygoster* originated. The word may be derived from the German *schnelle geister*, meaning "quick spirit," but extravagant nonsense words such as *lollapalooza* and *splendiferous* were popular during the nineteenth century. *Snollygoster* may simply be part of this trend.

Snollygoster, although nearly obsolete, enjoyed a brief moment of celebrity in 2009 when British politician Richard Graham used it on his website. After a flap over questionable campaign expenditures, Graham challenged his opponent to publish his expenses "so that all Gloucester voters could see that he isn't a snollygoster."

1888

BENJAMIN HARRISON (REPUBLICAN) VS. GROVER CLEVELAND (DEMOCRAT)

The Beast of Buffalo

Although Grover Cleveland was unmarried when he entered the White House, soon afterward he married Frances Folsom, the twenty-one-year-old daughter of his old law partner. Cleveland was forty-nine. This event provided the Republicans with the small handful of dirt that they were able to fling during the 1888 presidential campaign. Labeling Cleveland the Beast of Buffalo, they spread the rumor that he beat his young wife in fits of drunken rage. Americans were appalled, especially because the First Lady was very well liked. Eventually Mrs. Cleveland felt compelled to issue a statement calling the rumor "a foolish campaign story without a shadow of foundation."

The 1888 election was otherwise a lackluster contest, centering on whether to lower the high tariffs, as Cleveland proposed, or leave them in place, as the Republicans wished. Cleveland ran into trouble when the English ambassador, Sir Lionel Sackville-West, was duped into writing a letter stating that Cleveland's position on the tariffs made him a more England-friendly candidate. This did not sit well with anti-British Americans, a large contingent in the late nineteenth century. Republicans kept the issue in the foreground by referring to Cleveland as the English Candidate.

Cleveland also hurt himself by refusing to campaign while occupying the White House. His Republican opponent Benjamin

Harrison (grandson of William Henry of Tippecanoe fame) ran a low-key but well-organized campaign that included squeezing impressive donations out of business owners who supported high tariffs. Although Cleveland received more popular votes, he lost badly in the electoral college. He would come back to beat Harrison in 1892, the only president to hold two nonconsecutive terms.

Wheel Horses and Ward Heelers

Party loyalty was important in the era of local machine politics. Party bosses may have been running the show, but they couldn't deliver the votes without the help of their faithful underlings.

Horses harnessed directly in front of the wagon or carriage wheels are called wheel horses. They follow the lead horses and do the heavy pulling. Party wheel horses are the staunch hardworking loyalists who can be counted on to keep their districts in line. In return they expect to feed at the public trough when their candidate wins.

Figurative uses of *wheel horse* first appeared in the 1860s. An early example comes from an article about local politics in the *Weekly New Mexican* for August 24, 1867: "Carleton . . . worked like a beaver for Perea, and so did Perfecto Armijo, the Perea wheel horse in that county then." The term died out in the early twentieth century, along with horse-drawn vehicles.

If wheel horses pull the political wagon, ward heelers are more like faithful canine companions. They stick close to the heels of ward bosses—politicians who work at the local level. (A ward has been the basic American political district since colonial times.)

Like wheel horses, ward heelers are expected to get out the votes for their candidate.

The earliest use of *ward heeler* is found in the *Quarterly Review* of July 1890: "The lowest grade [of politician] is the 'ward heeler,' or hanger-on of the political head of the city ward in which he resides." Ward heelers tend to be disreputable. Theodore Roosevelt lumps them with other shady political types in an 1890 article in the *Century*: "[Patronage] is among the most potent of the many forces which combine to produce the ward boss, the district heeler, the boodle alderman." The term *ward heeler* is not heard as often since the decline of powerful political machines such as Tammany Hall.

1892

GROVER CLEVELAND (DEMOCRAT) VS. BENJAMIN HARRISON (REPUBLICAN) VS. JAMES B. WEAVER (POPULIST)

The 1892 election was even quieter than that of 1888. Harrison did not campaign because his wife, who died two weeks before the election, was seriously ill with tuberculosis. Cleveland also kept a low profile, out of respect for the First Lady. The main issue was once again the tariff. The Republicans favored it, believing it was necessary for the country's prosperity, while the Democrats considered it "a robbery of the great majority of the American people for the benefit of the few."

The only lively campaign belonged to the Populists, a recently formed party made up of southern and western farmers and laborers frustrated by their worsening economic situation. Their candidate, James B. Weaver, drew supporters with his fiery stump speeches attacking Wall Street and the bankers. Among the proposed Populist reforms were a graduated income tax, government ownership of railroads, and the free coinage of silver to put more money in circulation.

The most compelling incident of the campaign season occurred during the summer when the Carnegie Steel Company of Homestead, Pennsylvania, sharply reduced wages in a move to crush the union. The resulting violent clash between Carnegie and its workers—which Carnegie won—seriously damaged the Republican cause. Labor voters had been told that high tariffs brought prosperity, but Carnegie's actions showed that improved profits for factory owners did not necessarily mean gains for employees. Labor went heavily for Cleveland, giving him the election. Weaver earned twenty-two electoral votes, impressive for a third-party candidate, but not enough to affect the outcome.

1896

WILLIAM McKINLEY (REPUBLICAN) VS. WILLIAM JENNINGS BRYAN (DEMOCRAT/ POPULIST)

Goldbugs, Straddlebugs, and Silverites

The 1896 campaign was all about money. The financial excesses of the late nineteenth century culminated in the Panic of 1893, during which numerous banks and railroads failed. Millions were suddenly unemployed and farm prices fell.

A few years earlier, the government had started purchasing silver to soak up the flood of oversupply from western silver mines. The treasury bought the silver with specially issued notes that could be redeemed for either silver or gold. As a result of investors redeeming them for gold, the country's gold reserves dropped dangerously low. After the panic, President Cleveland stopped the government's silver buying in an effort to build up the gold supply and to curb inflation. The value of silver dropped dramatically. Besides putting silver mines out of business, the dearth of currency exacerbated the money problems of debtors and the poor.

The 1896 presidential campaign was fought between those who believed in a gold standard for currency—the Goldbugs—and those who supported the free coinage of silver—the Silverites. Goldbugs tended to be investors and business owners, while Silverites were mainly farmers and other workers who would benefit from increased money circulation. Those who waffled on the issue were called Straddlebugs. Some newspapers thought that this group included the Republican nominee, William McKinley, but by the time of the campaign he was a committed Goldbug.

The king of the Silverites was Democratic presidential candidate William Jennings Bryan. Bryan electrified the convention with his memorable "Cross of Gold" speech. Arguing that small merchants, farmers, and miners deserved equal consideration with "financial magnates," he concluded his speech ringingly: "[Y]ou shall not press down upon the brow of labor this crown of thorns. You shall not crucify mankind upon a cross of gold." When Bryan finished, the enraptured audience went wild. The Populist Party, which had championed the cause of "free silver" in 1892, also chose Bryan as their candidate.

Bryan was a magnificent speaker, good-looking and charismatic. Thirty-six years old at the time, he is still the youngest presidential candidate ever nominated by a major party. Bryan traveled thousands of miles around the country and made over six hundred speeches during the campaign. Everywhere he went, he preached the gospel of free silver.

Realizing that they could not compete with Bryan on the stump, the Republicans evolved a "front porch" campaign for McKinley, who received a steady stream of visitors at his Ohio home. They touted McKinley as the candidate of prosperity and sound money. They also went negative against Bryan, attacking his free silver policy as reckless and deluded. One of their slogans was "In God we trust / With Bryan we bust." They also issued fake anti-Bryan coins. One had Bryan's picture on one side and "In God we trust . . . for the other 47 cents" inscribed on the other side. Another fake coin said, "From the silver mines of Bunco state."

The Republicans also used a tactic that would reappear in future campaigns. They attacked Bryan on what many considered his strongest point—his emotion-laden speaking style. They claimed that it showed he was mentally unstable. On September 27, 1896, the *New York Times* published an outrageous piece titled "Is Bryan Crazy?" The editorial summarized the views of an unnamed psychiatrist who had concluded that the candidate's speeches were not the utterances of a sane person, based on their "progressive recklessness and vanity." The author points out that Bryan is stumping in the Northeast, where he doesn't have a hope of winning, saying, "His procedures are not intelligent means to intelligible ends." He believes that Bryan is simply satiating his overweening vanity.

On the same page, the paper published a letter from another psychiatrist, who said, "Mr. Bryan presents in speech and action striking and alarming evidence of a mind not entirely sound." This doctor concluded that Bryan suffered from megalomania.

Bryan lost by about half a million votes. By the time of the election, the economy was improving and the issue of free silver was less compelling than it had been. Bryan would run unsuccessfully two more times, in 1900 and 1908, before abandoning his presidential hopes. Today he is best known as prosecuting council during the 1925 Scopes Monkey Trial over the teaching of evolution.

Two factors that influenced the 1896 election would become increasingly central to elections in the next century. The first was the sharp political divide between the agricultural South and West and the industrial North and Midwest. The second was the power of campaign spending. The McKinley campaign raised several million dollars to Bryan's three hundred thousand. Candidates with the most financial muscle still get to fling the most mud.

★ 4 ★

The Lunatic Fringe

THE AGE OF REFORM, WORLD WAR I, AND THE 1920s

1900–1928

By the turn of the twentieth century, memories of the Civil War were beginning to fade and Americans looked to the future. Political struggles centered around which direction the country would take—imperialism or, as Teddy Roosevelt put it, "contraction"; isolationism or entanglement in European conflicts; corporate piracy or the socialist fringe.

The 1898 Spanish-American War, giving the United States control of Puerto Rico, Guam, and the Philippines, was widely considered "a splendid little war"—Teddy's words again—but in 1914 Americans resisted being drawn into Europe's bloody conflict. Woodrow Wilson captured a second term with the prematurely congratulatory slogan "He kept us out of war." On the home front, reforming journalists crusaded against corporate monopolies, but the other side of the coin was increasing hysteria over "the Red Menace."

Theodore Roosevelt looms large over the reform era. He invented several negative terms of this period, including *malefactors of great wealth* and *lunatic fringe*. In spite of his way with words, he was seldom the victim of retaliatory mud, protected by his forthright character and huge popularity with voters. Not that mudslinging was dead—far from it. The vicious 1928 attacks waged on Catholic presidential candidate Al Smith equaled or exceeded previous negative campaigns.

1900

WILLIAM McKINLEY (REPUBLICAN) VS. WILLIAM JENNINGS BRYAN (DEMOCRAT)

That Madman on the Ticket

The 1900 contest was a replay of 1896, but with less noise. Both parties nominated their candidates on the first ballot. The only convention excitement came from the selection of Theodore Roosevelt as the Republican vice presidential candidate. Roosevelt, who was governor of New York, was drafted onto the Republican ticket mostly through the enthusiasm of the delegates. They revered him for his exploits as a Rough Rider during the Spanish-American War, including the famous charge up San Juan Hill.

Roosevelt was much less popular, however, among party insiders. Republican National Committee chair Mark Hanna fought to keep him off the ticket. Hanna thought the Rough Rider aspects of Roosevelt's character made him too volatile for a vice presidential candidate. Trying to convince party leaders to make another choice, he cried, "Don't any of you realize that there's only one life between that madman and the presidency?" His words were prescient.

The two candidates revived the issues of four years earlier. Bryan continued to attack big business and call for a policy of free silver. He also spoke out against what he saw as America's quest for an empire. Having liberated the Philippines from Spain during the Spanish-American War, the United States was currently fighting the Filipinos themselves to keep control of the islands.

McKinley left most of the stumping to Roosevelt, whose talents in that line equaled Bryan's. Roosevelt traveled around the country, speaking passionately in defense of America's actions in the Philippines. Voters tended to agree. Most still approved of Roosevelt's "splendid little" Spanish-American War. Nor were they moved by the free silver issue, which seemed irrelevant in the upbeat economy of the time. With Roosevelt's help, McKinley easily won another four years.

1904

THEODORE ROOSEVELT (REPUBLICAN) VS. ALTON PARKER (DEMOCRAT)

His Accidency

Mark Hanna's worst fears were realized on September 6, 1901, when an anarchist shot President McKinley at the Pan-American Exposition in Buffalo, New York. He died eight days later, and Roosevelt assumed the presidency. Hanna was bitter about the turn of events. H. H. Kohlsaat, editor of the *Chicago Times-Herald*, recalls speaking with him on McKinley's funeral train. Hanna fumed, "I told William McKinley it was a mistake to nominate that wild man at Philadelphia. . . . Now look, that damned cowboy is president of the United States."

Those dismayed by "that wild man's" ascent to the presidency referred to him as His Accidency. This dismissive phrase was first applied to John Tyler when he inherited the presidency from William Henry Harrison in 1841. *Accidency* is a rarely used word for a chance happening.

Roosevelt deeply resented this title. He was determined to run again and be elected in his own right. The Republican leadership would have preferred a more conventional candidate, but the voters loved his unorthodox style. The *New York Sun* expressed what many people felt about him with their famously succinct, backhanded endorsement. The five-word editorial declared: "Theodore! With all thy faults."

The 1904 election was fairly colorless. Roosevelt adhered to the principle that sitting presidents don't campaign. His opponent Alton Parker, chief justice of the New York Court of Appeals, was a deeply reserved man who didn't travel and made only a handful of campaign speeches. He couldn't begin to compete with the popular Roosevelt. Parker carried only thirteen states, all of them in the South.

On election night, when the returns showed that Roosevelt had won an overwhelming victory, the president turned to his wife and remarked, "My dear, I am no longer a political accident." He was still savoring his triumph a few days later when Republican politician Joseph Benson Foraker called to pay his respects. Foraker recalls in his memoirs, "When I was ushered into his office he walked forward briskly to shake hands and welcome me. In doing so he announced with manifest satisfaction, 'You are shaking hands with His Excellency, not His Accidency.'"

The Millionaire's Club

The nickname the Millionaire's Club for the U.S. Senate arose in the 1890s, when $1 million represented considerably more wealth than it does now. The press popularized it during Roosevelt's fight to regulate the railroads. The prevalence of tightly organized political machines during the late nineteenth and early twentieth centuries made it easy for wealthy men to buy their way into a Senate seat.

Activist journalists saw these men as "the puppets of privileged wealth," doubting whether they would be willing or able to regulate big business. The November 28, 1901, issue of Missouri's *Moberly Weekly Monitor* says, "Great corporations have found it to be a good investment to put one of their number . . . into a congressional seat. . . . The Senate has recently been called 'The Millionaire's Club.'"

This perception may not have been entirely accurate. A few years earlier the *Newark Daily Advocate* pointed out that although the Senate was commonly known as the Millionaire's Club, this label really fit only members from the North. "As a rule," the paper assured readers, "senators from the south and west are in moderate circumstances."

Loose Cannon

Roosevelt had no sooner taken office in 1901 than he began to worry about what he would do when his term was over. After a small dinner one evening at his brother-in-law's house, he began to speculate on what his future life would hold. He confided to his friends, "I don't want to be the old cannon loose on the deck in the storm."

The popularity of this phrase is usually credited to Roosevelt, but *loose cannon* was already known as a metaphor for an uncontrollable person or thing, especially one liable to cause damage. The image probably comes from Victor Hugo's description of a cannon rolling loose on a ship's deck in his 1874 novel *Ninety-Three*: "A cannon which breaks its moorings . . . is a machine which transforms itself into a monster. . . . You can reason with a bull-dog, astonish a bull, fascinate a boa, frighten a tiger, soften a lion; no resource with such a monster as a loose cannon."

The phrase *loose cannon* faded in popularity after Roosevelt's day, but came back into vogue in the late 1970s as a metaphor for an unpredictable or out-of-control politician. These days the term is often used to refer to someone who can't be relied on to vote the party line.

Malefactors of Great Wealth

Roosevelt was committed to reining in corporate excesses. He coined *malefactors of great wealth* to refer to both corporate entities and individuals who made their money unethically. He used the term frequently. A typical example comes from a 1909 essay titled "The Thraldom of Names," written for the *Outlook*: "The big newspaper, owned or controlled in Wall Street, . . . which is quite willing to hound politicians for their misdeeds, but which with raving fury defends all the malefactors of great wealth." While in office he often spoke out—and took action—against monied interests.

The label *malefactors of great wealth* was revived in 2009, thanks to Wall Street high jinks that came to a head that year. The phrase appeared in dozens of newspaper articles and op-ed pieces. One example is Bob Herbert's *New York Times* column of July 13, 2009: "These malefactors of great wealth (thank you, Teddy) developed hideously destructive credit policies and took insane risks that hurt millions of American families and nearly wrecked the economy."

Muckrakers

Investigative journalists prodded Roosevelt into some of the reforms that occurred during his presidency. For instance, Upton Sinclair's sensational 1906 novel, *The Jungle*, exposed the corruption and horrendous working conditions of the meatpacking industry. Roosevelt's support of the Pure Food and Drug Act was partly a response to the public outcry following the book's publication.

Roosevelt had some ambivalence about dirt-digging journalists. In a 1906 speech he says, "In Bunyan's *Pilgrim's Progress* you may recall the description of the man with the muck-rake, . . . who was offered a celestial crown for his muck-rake, but who would neither look up nor regard the crown he was offered, but continued to rake to himself the filth of the floor." Roosevelt concludes by saying, "[T]he men with the muck rakes are often indispensable to the wellbeing of society, but only if they know when to stop raking the muck."

Muckraker soon entered the language as a name for someone who digs for and exposes corruption. It's also used pejoratively to describe a tell-all journalist who revels in scandal and sensationalism.

1908

WILLIAM TAFT (REPUBLICAN) VS. WILLIAM JENNINGS BRYAN (DEMOCRAT)

Rum, Romanism, and Capitalism

In 1908 William Jennings Bryan made his final run for the presidency. He abandoned the now-defunct cause of free silver and ran with the anticorporate theme "Shall the people rule?" His Republican opponent was Roosevelt's hand-picked successor, William Taft. The Republicans would have preferred the still wildly popular Roosevelt as their candidate, but the president had already announced his determination not to run again.

In the beginning, Taft was a lackluster campaigner who gave boring, statistics-filled speeches. Roosevelt coached him energetically. In one letter, he advises, "Do not answer Bryan; *attack* him. Don't let him make the issues." Roosevelt also told Taft, "Let the audience see you smile always."

Taft enjoyed playing golf, but his mentor disapproved. "Photographs on horseback, yes," he wrote, "tennis, no, and golf is fatal." Later, Roosevelt changed his mind about the 290-pound Taft appearing on horseback, declaring it was "dangerous to him and cruelty to the horse." Roosevelt's unsubtle attempts to direct Taft's campaign gave rise to suggestions that the candidate was simply the president's mouthpiece. One joke had it that T.A.F.T. stood for "Take advice from Theodore."

Taft was also criticized for belonging to the Unitarian Church, just as John Quincy Adams had been a century earlier. A letter in the *Pentecostal Herald* exclaims, "Think of the United States with a president who does not believe that Jesus Christ is the son of God, but looks upon our Immaculate Savior as a common bastard and low, cunning imposter." Others suggested that Taft was too friendly with the Catholic Church. He had worked closely with church officials while governor-general of the Philippines.

William Jennings Bryan's main enemies came from the corporate world that he so vigorously attacked. They claimed that economic disaster would follow a Bryan win, while support for Taft would guarantee continued prosperity. One campaign poster asks voters, "Which do you prefer? Bryan and Bones or Taft and Turkey?"

Some businesses went to the length of making sure there really was prosperity, at least until the election. Managers of the New York Central Railroad ordered repairs to twenty-five hundred of their cars, whether needed or not, so they could temporarily employ more people. Republicans also made a joke of Bryan's repeated tries for the presidency with the slogan "Vote for Taft now, you can vote for Bryan anytime."

Roosevelt's cascade of advice apparently worked because Taft handed Bryan his worst defeat to date, winning 321 electoral votes to Bryan's 162. Bryan was shocked and puzzled by his loss. He invited readers of the *Commoner*, the magazine he edited, to write in with their analysis of why the campaign had failed. Many who responded blamed an unholy conspiracy of anti-Prohibitionists, Catholics, and big capital, using catchphrases such as "Rum, Romanism, and Capitalism" and "Catholicism, Commercialism, and Coercion." Many believed the false rumor that instructions to vote for Taft had been read out from Catholic pulpits on the Sunday before the election.

The *Rum/Romanism* theme taps into a powerful substrate in American politics—prejudice against Catholic candidates. In 1856 Frémont was smeared with accusations of a "Romish Intrigue," and in 1884 James G. Blaine's supporters slapped the *Rum, Romanism, and Rebellion* label on the Democrats. Yet another version of this negative slogan would surface during Al Smith's run for the presidency in 1928.

1912

WOODROW WILSON (DEMOCRAT) VS. WILLIAM TAFT (REPUBLICAN) VS. THEODORE ROOSEVELT (BULL MOOSE) VS. EUGENE DEBS (SOCIALIST)

A Dead Cock in a Pit

The nastiest dirt during the 1912 presidential campaign was thrown between the two top Republicans. By the time of the election, Roosevelt was thoroughly disenchanted with his former friend Taft, feeling that the president had betrayed the Progressive Republican platform. American voters were also disappointed in the Taft administration. They showed it by voting for Democrats during the midterm elections.

Roosevelt decided that to save his party he must abandon his vow not to run again. "My hat is in the ring," he announced. "The fight is on and I am stripped to the buff!" Taft, hurt and furious, went on the attack. In a speech before the Republican Club of New York, he lashed out against "political emotionalists or neurotics . . . who seek . . . to reconstruct society on new principles." He predicted that if the Progressive wing of the party triumphed, the country would plunge into anarchy.

Roosevelt came out swinging. In an answering speech, he says of Taft, "I do not believe he has given the people a square deal. . . .

He has yielded to the bosses and to the great privileged interests." He adds unkindly, "I think he means well; but he means well feebly." Roosevelt reminded Taft that Taft was president only because Roosevelt supported him in 1908.

Taft was reluctant to call Roosevelt names in public, but privately he compared his old mentor to a fakir at the head of a religious cult. He wrote to his wife, "He is seeking to make his followers 'Holy Rollers' . . . I look upon him as I look upon a freak." Roosevelt had no qualms about publicly insulting Taft. He likened his opponent to "a dead cock in a pit" and "a fathead with the brains of a guinea pig."

Roosevelt challenged Taft in the primaries and won nine states against Taft's one, including Taft's home state of Ohio. However, Taft controlled the party machinery, and delegates from the state conventions were committed to him. These advantages allowed him to capture the nomination.

Roosevelt and his supporters staged their own raucous nominating convention two months later. The crowd gave Roosevelt a fifty-two-minute ovation when he appeared on the meeting hall stage. As they cheered and stood on their chairs, he cried, "We stand at Armageddon and we battle for the Lord!" Before the 1900 campaign, Roosevelt had bragged that he was "as strong as a bull moose," so the breakaway Republicans named themselves the Bull Moose Party. In a more sedate nominating convention, the Democrats chose New Jersey governor and former Princeton president Woodrow Wilson.

The campaign was relatively low key after the excitement of

the primaries. Wilson and Roosevelt were the only two candidates who counted. The easygoing Taft sidelined himself, telling newsmen, "I have been told that I ought to do this, ought to do that . . . that I do not keep myself in the headlines . . . but I can't do it." A fourth candidate, Socialist Eugene V. Debs, was not a serious electoral threat. As there were few major differences between the parties' platforms, the contest was mainly one of personalities—the boisterous Roosevelt versus the austere Wilson.

Roosevelt's critics focused on his arrogance in running for a third term. Although no rule demanded it, presidents were expected to follow George Washington's example and retire gracefully after serving two terms. One Democratic congressman read an anti-Roosevelt poem received from a constituent into the *Congressional Record*. It begins, "I'm twice as great as Washington, / I'm twice as great as Grant, / Because third terms they didn't get, / They needn't think I can't."

Roosevelt tried to finesse the issue by explaining that when he said he would not run for a third term, he meant a third consecutive term. In a February 17, 1908, commentary, the *Outlook* joked, "When a man says at breakfast in the morning, 'No, thank you, I will not take any more coffee,' it does not mean that he will not take any more coffee tomorrow morning, or next week, or next month, or next year."

Wilson himself refrained from making personal attacks on Roosevelt, concentrating instead on presenting his proposals for financial and industrial reform. Nor was he the target of any serious mud. Although stories of his relationship with the socialite

Mary Hulbert Peck were beginning to surface, they did not become widely known until the next election.

The most dramatic moment of the campaign came on the evening of October 14, when a man rushed up to Roosevelt as he was about to enter a Milwaukee auditorium. Shouting out something about third terms, he shot Roosevelt in the chest. True to his "bull moose" reputation, Roosevelt insisted on giving his speech before being taken to the hospital. Pulling bloodstained notes out of his coat pocket, he talked for an hour and a half.

Roosevelt used the opportunity to take a swipe at his opponents, telling the agape audience, "It is a natural thing that weak and violent minds should be inflamed . . . by the kind of artful mendacity and abuse that have been heaped upon me for the last three months." Later X-rays showed that the bullet had lodged in Roosevelt's powerful chest muscles, luckily missing his lung.

The 1912 election was to be the American public's last taste of Roosevelt-style campaign drama. Although Wilson did not win a majority of popular votes, the Republican Party's split guaranteed a Democratic victory in the electoral college. Most Bull Moosers, including the former president, returned to the Republicans after the election.

The Lunatic Fringe

Lunatic fringe is another of Theodore Roosevelt's memorable contributions to the language, although he first used it to talk about art rather than politics. In a review of the New York City Armory's 1913 exhibit of modernist art, he wrote, "We have to face the fact that there is apt to be a lunatic fringe among the votaries of any forward movement. In this recent art exhibition the lunatic fringe was fully in evidence, especially in the rooms devoted to the Cubists and Futurists."

Lunatic fringe was quickly adopted as a political term. One writer who chronicled Roosevelt's own Bull Moose convention remembers, "Among those highly wrought individualists, the delegates . . . the 'lunatic fringe' was often plainly in view."

When Roosevelt coined *lunatic fringe*, *lunatic* was still a medical term for a mentally ill person. Since the mid-twentieth century, the word is used only symbolically. The lunatic fringe these days can be located on either the left or right edge of the political spectrum, depending on your point of view.

1916

Woodrow Wilson (Democrat) vs. Charles Hughes (Republican)

Peck's Bad Boy

President Wilson's approval rating was high when the next election came around because he had kept the United States out of Europe's war. He ran against the Republican candidate, former New York governor Charles Hughes, on the slogan "Wilson and peace with honor, / Or Hughes with Roosevelt and war." Roosevelt, once again fully engaged with the Republicans, was causing problems for Hughes with his fiercely pro-war stance.

As the campaign progressed, it became clear that Hughes was struggling to walk a line between the isolationism of most Americans and the hawkishness of Roosevelt and other pro-war Republicans. He was forced to tailor his message depending on the audience, earning him the nickname Charles Evasive Hughes. (His middle name was Evans.)

Hughes also made the mistake of snubbing California governor Hiram Johnson, a fellow Republican running for reelection. When the two were staying at the same Long Beach hotel late in the campaign, Hughes neglected to arrange a meeting with Johnson. Hughes later claimed that he didn't realize Johnson was in the hotel, but the damage was done. Johnson withheld his support, with the eventual result that Hughes lost California to Wilson.

Given these blunders, Wilson concluded that he could safely ignore Hughes during the campaign. He explained to a friend, "Never murder a man who is committing suicide."

The president's foreign policy was popular, but some Americans were unhappy about his personal life. Wilson was married when he entered the White House. His wife, Ellen, died of kidney disease in August 1914, and just one year later he married Edith Bolling Galt, a forty-two-year-old widow. Many were shocked by what they considered his unseemly haste. Whispers began to circulate that Wilson and Mrs. Galt were romantically involved before the first Mrs. Wilson died, and that she died of a broken heart. A more sensational story claimed that Wilson had actually caused his wife's death by pushing her down stairs.

The rumors linking Wilson with Mary Hulbert Peck also resurfaced at this time and became more widespread. Mrs. Peck was divorced when Wilson met her in 1910 while vacationing in Bermuda without his wife. It's unclear whether the two had an affair, but Wilson was obviously infatuated for a time. He poured out his thoughts to her in many intense, intimate letters. Gossip had it that Peck threatened to publish the letters until Wilson's friend, the lawyer Louis Brandeis, paid her off. Brandeis called this tale "a vile slander."

Nonetheless, President Wilson acquired the nickname Peck's Bad Boy. The name refers to a series of stories by George W. Peck, featuring a mischievous young boy named Henry Peck. The most popular compilation was *Peck's Bad Boy and His Pa*, published in 1883. Wilson complained bitterly that it was impossible to respond directly to "these fiendish lies," but his campaign managers tried to counteract them. They had Wilson's former brother-in-law write a biographical sketch titled "Mr. Wilson as Seen by One of His Family Circle," portraying the president as a devoted family man.

The election was close—Hughes carried nearly all of the eastern and midwestern states—but Wilson's isolationist stance won the day. Unfortunately, the world situation changed shortly after the election. Germany began attacking all ships found in the war zones, even those flying neutral flags. In April 1917, after German submarines sank several American merchant ships, Congress declared war.

Parlor Pinks

The Russian Revolution of 1917 triggered the first Red Scare—American fears of the socialists, or reds, in their midst. Socialist Party candidate Eugene Debs garnered nearly 6 percent of the vote in 1912, but the party's reputation suffered when socialists spoke out against the war. Politicians and newspaper editors began railing against the pervasive threat of American reds and their sympathizers, the pinks.

Theodore Roosevelt inspired the term *parlor pink*. He writes of *parlor bolshevism* in his 1918 book about World War I, *The Great Adventure*: "Our own moral fiber is weakened by the parlor or pink-tea or sissy Bolshevism." (Communists were called Bolsheviks until the mid-twentieth century, from a Russian word that translates loosely as "majority.") Roosevelt distinguished parlor bolshevism—advocating socialism in the safety of one's parlor—from the more violent "gutter bolshevism" of the truly committed. By 1920 *parlor bolshevism* had evolved into the snappier term *parlor pink*, as in this sentence from the *Ironwood (MI) Daily Globe* for January 27, 1920: "Violent reds can be deported but the parlor pinks are a more persistent nuisance."

Parlor pinks disappeared along with parlors, but *pink* and *pinko* are still current. Similar terms, more familiar today, are *armchair leftist* and *limousine liberal* (see Chapter 8).

1920

WARREN G. HARDING (REPUBLICAN) VS. JAMES COX (DEMOCRAT)

Happy Hooligan

By 1920 Americans were weary of Wilsonism, especially Wilson's long, losing struggle to sell the League of Nations to a resistant Congress. Voters were ready for a change. They got it with the Republican candidate, Warren G. Harding. In contrast to the reserved, intellectual Wilson, Harding was outgoing and genial, but hardly a deep thinker. Owner of a small-town Ohio newspaper, Harding was currently serving in the Senate. One Republican colleague characterized him as "the best of the second raters."

The Democrats nominated Ohio governor James Cox. Cox promised Wilson, who had recently suffered a stroke, that he would keep up the fight to bring the United States into the League.

Cox dubbed Harding Happy Hooligan, after a comic strip character of the time. Happy Hooligan was a happy-go-lucky hobo who didn't let his many misfortunes get him down. He just kept on smiling. Harding was equally easygoing, content to let party bigwigs run the campaign.

Harding's open, friendly manner overcame a number of personal negatives. He chewed tobacco, played cards, and made no secret of enjoying his whiskey, in spite of the recently passed Eighteenth Amendment outlawing alcoholic beverages. Riskiest of all for a presidential candidate, he indulged in mistresses. The Republicans headed off disaster by sending Harding's latest mistress and her husband on a fact-finding tour of Asia that would last until after the election.

Harding's main weakness was his tendency to "bloviate," as he himself called it (see Chapter 1 for more on this word). One prominent Democrat described Harding's speeches as "an army of pompous phrases moving across the landscape in search of an idea." Harding was given to speaking in pleasant-sounding generalities. Early in the campaign he declared, "America's present need is . . . not nostrums but normalcy." *Normalcy*, an established word but rarely used before Harding, sounded strange to journalists covering the event. They jumped on it as evidence of Harding's loose grasp of standard English.

H. L. Mencken, who later wrote *The American Language*, was especially severe. Mencken declared that Harding wrote the worst English he had ever encountered, saying it reminded him of "a string of wet sponges; . . . of tattered washing on the line; . . . of dogs barking idiotically through endless nights. It is so bad that a sort of grandeur creeps into it." He pointed to such mistakes as Harding's use of *civic* for *civil*, *luring* for *alluring*, and *referendum* for *reference*.

The most potentially damaging attack on Harding came in the form of a whispering campaign about his ancestry. The rumors may have originated with his father-in-law, who hated him, or with the editor of a rival newspaper in his hometown. Flyers began appearing that suggested Harding had one or more black ancestors. An Ohio college professor named Chancellor authored a pamphlet in which he claimed to have traced Harding's family tree back to a West Indian man. Given the racial intolerance of the 1920s, such a claim, if widely believed, could easily have cost Harding the election.

The rumors did not get the exposure they might have because Wilson forbade the Democrats to touch the issue. He directed postal authorities to confiscate copies of the pamphlet before they could be disseminated through the mail. Newspapers, for the most part, also left the story alone. Only one intrepid *Cincinnati Enquirer* reporter questioned Harding on the truth of the matter. He responded with typical good humor that he didn't know—one of his ancestors "may have jumped the fence."

The Republican Party never mentioned the topic directly. They simply circulated pictures of Harding's blue-eyed parents and diagrams of his European family tree, to the puzzlement of those not in the know.

Harding did not bother to campaign against Cox. Voters were so disenchanted with the Democratic Party's dogged support of the League of Nations that Harding's victory was ensured. He swept into office with a landmark majority—a whopping 60 percent of the vote. He carried every state outside the South, plus Tennessee.

1924

CALVIN COOLIDGE (REPUBLICAN) VS. JOHN DAVIS (DEMOCRAT)

Silent Cal

When Harding died suddenly in 1923 he was succeeded by Vice President Calvin Coolidge. Coolidge then ran for his own term in 1924. Harding left behind several messy political scandals, most notably the Teapot Dome affair, in which the secretary of the interior awarded leases to government-owned oil fields in return for bribes. These scandals had little negative effect on Coolidge. The Vermonter was the picture of stern New England rectitude.

Coolidge also displayed another Yankee trait—taciturnity. He was known to friends and foes alike as Silent Cal. During the campaign, several stories made the rounds. One anecdote, possibly apocryphal, told of a young woman seated next to Coolidge at a dinner. She pertly informed him that a friend had bet her Coolidge wouldn't say three words all evening. "You lose," he replied, then turned back to his plate. The writer Dorothy Parker, when told of Coolidge's death in 1933, quipped, "How could they tell?"

The Republicans did not consider Silent Cal's low-key style a negative. They praised it as evidence of his no-nonsense approach to governing. During the nominating convention, one of the seconders, fellow Vermonter William W. Stickney, said of the Coolidge family in general that they "never wasted any time, never wasted any words, and never wasted any public money."

Nervous Nellie

The dismissive nickname Nervous Nellie originally belonged to Frank B. Kellogg, Minnesota's Republican senator from 1917 to 1923. The name first appeared in newspapers when Kellogg was appointed secretary of state in 1925, although he acquired it during his time in the Senate. One of the earliest mentions in print comes from the *New York Herald Tribune* for January 11, 1925: "[Kellogg] was labeled 'Nervous Nellie' by those who were irritated at his maneuvering during the League of Nations fight." When Kellogg was first being called Nervous Nellie, *nelly* was slang for an effeminate man, so the label would have carried a suggestion of sissiness.

Kellogg was one of the few Republicans to support the League of Nations but is best known for his sponsorship of the 1928 Kellogg-Briand Pact. Signed by sixty-three countries, the pact renounces the use of war as "an instrument of national policy." He received the 1929 Nobel Peace Prize in recognition of this effort. Eventually Kellogg's association with *Nervous Nellie* was forgot-

---

Nervous Nellie is often still used to label those reluctant to go to war. In a statement quoted in *Time* for May 27, 1966, President Lyndon Johnson said, referring to the escalating Vietnam War, "The road ahead is going to be difficult. There will be some Nervous Nellies." President George W. Bush also used the term in 2002, saying, "There's a lot of nervous nellies at the Pentagon."

---

ten, and it entered the language as a general term for an overly timid person or a worry wart.

1928

HERBERT HOOVER (REPUBLICAN) VS. AL SMITH (DEMOCRAT)

Rum, Romanism, and Tammany

On August 2, 1927, while at his vacation home in South Dakota's Black Hills, Silent Cal stepped out to waiting reporters. He handed one a slip of paper with the words, "I do not choose to run for president in 1928." Then he silently stepped back into the house.

Republicans turned instead to Herbert Hoover, the well-respected secretary of commerce. Hoover was a former mining engineer known for his competence in organizing European relief efforts during the war. He promised to run the country as a sensible businessman, continuing the policies that had brought the country "Coolidge Prosperity."

The Democratic nominee, Alfred E. Smith, provided voters with a sharply different choice. An Irish Catholic from New York's Lower East Side, he began his working life at the age of thirteen at Fulton's Fish Market. He rose to the governorship of New York with support from Tammany Hall.

It soon became apparent that voters outside the urban Northeast found Smith objectionable for a number of reasons unrelated to his campaign platform. His close association with Tammany

Hall, which for many Americans was synonymous with political corruption, was a decided negative, and his working-class background was a subject for ridicule. A remark overheard at the Southampton Republican Ladies caucus was typical: "I knew by his looks and his accent which party he belonged to." When Smith gave radio speeches, his heavy New York accent grated on listeners in other parts of the country.

Smith's wife, Kate, who had grown up in the same neighborhood as her husband, was subjected to similar insults. Mrs. Florence T. Griswold of the Republican National Committee amused her audience during one speech by inviting them to imagine "an aristocratic foreign ambassador" saying to Mrs. Smith, "What a charming gown," and the reply, "You said a mouthful!" Others sneered that the White House would reek of corned beef, cabbage, and "home brew" if she were to live there.

The most serious charges against Smith concerned rum and Romanism. Sales of alcoholic beverages had been illegal since 1920 with passage of the Eighteenth Amendment, which prohibited "the manufacture, sale or transportation of intoxicating liquors." By 1928, many politicians privately recognized that Prohibition was a failure—Americans consumed oceans of bootleg liquor every year—but its supporters were still powerful. Hoover, a committed "dry," gained their loyalty by calling the Eighteenth Amendment "a noble experiment." Smith, on the other hand, was a "wet." He believed the states should be allowed to make their own liquor laws and had come out in favor of repealing the Eighteenth Amendment.

Prohibitionist groups began to spread stories about "Alcoholic" Smith. One supposed eyewitness account claimed he had been so drunk at the New York State Fair that he needed two men to hold him upright. Smith tried to counteract such tales with witnesses of his own, but without success. The mere fact that he did not wholeheartedly support Prohibition was enough to condemn him in many minds as "rum-soaked."

The most virulent abuse, however, was reserved for Smith's Catholicism. Protestant preachers thundered denunciations from the pulpit. "If you vote for Al Smith," warned one, "you're voting against Christ and you'll be damned." Popular evangelist John Roach Straton preached over the radio on "Al Smith and the Forces of Hell." He lambasted Smith as a proponent of card playing, cocktail drinking, divorces, dancing, evolution, nude art, prize-fighting, and other modern horrors. A flurry of leaflets appeared with titles such as "Rum, Romanism, and Ruin," "Rum, Romanism, and Tammany," "Three Keys to Hell," and "A Vote for Al Smith Is a Vote for the Pope."

Denominational newspapers splashed lurid warnings across their front pages. One ran the headline, "Rome Suggests That Pope May Move Here." Another alerted readers that if Smith were elected, "the Romish system will institute persecutions again, and put the cruel, blood-stained heel upon all who refuse her authority." A third lumped together Catholics, political demagogues, brewers, bootleggers, and prostitutes, calling them all "the devil's crowd."

The absurdity of the rumors often reached a level that would have been laughable had their intent not been so serious. One story claimed that the newly built Holland Tunnel between Manhattan and Jersey City crossed under the ocean and emerged in the base-ment of the Vatican. Another said that all Protestant marriages would be annulled if Smith were elected.

Smith made some attempt to battle this outpouring of bigotry. When he traveled by campaign train across the West—with the newly resurgent Ku Klux Klan burning crosses along the tracks— he stopped in Oklahoma City to give a talk on religious tolerance. This move to tackle the subject head-on backfired. The audience, which included the Reverend Straton, was implacably hostile, and the Republicans criticized him for dragging religion into the campaign.

Hoover deplored the anti-Catholic slurs, but did little to re-press them. In fact, he never mentioned his opponent at all. He didn't need to. He simply positioned himself as the natural suc-cessor to Coolidge and Coolidge Prosperity. His promise of "a chicken in every pot and two cars in every garage" was enough to give him a landslide victory..

Sadly the economic boom times were about to end. Less than a year after the election, on October 24, 1929, the stock market crashed, ushering in the Great Depression. Hoover's approval rat-ings likewise took a plunge. No one would have predicted it in 1928, but he was destined to be a one-term president.

★ 5 ★

Hoovervilles and Bleeding Hearts

THE GREAT DEPRESSION AND WORLD WAR II

1932–1948

During the 1930s the economy overwhelmed all other political issues. When Herbert Hoover took office in 1929, times were good and the speculation craze was in full swing. Millions of Americans took advantage of easy credit plans to gamble on the bullish stock market. Then in late September, the market began to falter. Stock prices went into free fall as panicked investors started dumping shares. The crash came on Black Tuesday, October 29, when over sixteen million shares were traded, most at a fraction of their previous worth. People who were rich when they woke up that morning went to bed paupers.

As the economy sank into depression, Hoover's popularity also took a nosedive. By 1932, it seemed doubtful that he would be reelected. Instead, voters turned for rescue to the Democratic candidate, Franklin D. Roosevelt. Energetic and upbeat, Roosevelt gave Americans hope with his pledge of a "new deal." Once in office, he dominated government and politics for the next twelve years, winning reelection an unprecedented three times.

Although vastly popular, even FDR was not safe from mudslinging. Opponents of the New Deal attacked him as being little better than a communist. Others accused him of wanting to be a dictator or of scheming to drag the United States into another European war.

Hooverville

President Hoover at first refused to believe that the economic slump was serious. He was not alone—many economists assumed the stock market crash was nothing more than a necessary correction. However, as the months passed, and businesses continued to

---

The term *Hooverville* briefly made the news again after the economic downturn of 2008. The newly unemployed began congregating in makeshift camps outside large cities, usually in their cars or RVs, or occasionally in tents. Some news reporters borrowed the 1930s term to refer to these sites. For instance, an article posted online at the *San Francisco Sentinel* for February 28, 2009, is titled "The Return of Hooverville."

---

fail, millions lost their life savings, and 25 percent of the workforce lost their jobs, Hoover's continued optimism struck Americans as either foolish or callous. Statements like "the worst has passed" rang hollow to men tramping from town to town in search of work.

Hoover took steps to stimulate the economy, including the funding of public works projects. However, he remained adamantly opposed to monetary relief, believing that federal aid to individuals would weaken Americans' moral character. Men and women with hungry children to feed deeply resented this attitude. They began using Hoover's name to label all the miseries of the Great Depression.

The wretched shantytowns that sprang up on the edge of every city were known as Hoovervilles. Hoover flags were empty pockets, turned inside out in the vain hope of finding a stray coin. Hoover shoes featured cardboard linings to cover the holes in the soles. Newspapers that the homeless wrapped themselves in while sleeping outdoors were called Hoover blankets. Hoboes rode in freight cars dubbed Hoover Pullmans, rather than in genuine Pullman passenger cars. A "busted" flush in poker was nicknamed a Hoover flush.

Anti-Hoover slogans were numerous. Iowa farmers whose crops were nearly worthless originated the jingle "In Hoover we trusted, / Now we are busted." Alluding to the Hoover brand of vacuum cleaners, signs said, "Hoover cleaned us all" or "Hard times are still 'Hoovering' over us." The president's name was now synonymous with destitution.

1932

FRANKLIN D. ROOSEVELT (DEMOCRAT) VS. HERBERT HOOVER (REPUBLICAN)

The Kangaroo Ticket

Many Democratic Party chiefs considered New York governor Franklin D. Roosevelt a weak choice in 1932. He had run as James Cox's vice presidential candidate in 1920 but did not have the strong track record of some other presidential hopefuls, including Al Smith, who wanted to run again. It took four votes and aggressive behind-the-scenes maneuvering to get Roosevelt nominated.

H. L. Mencken commented, "Here was a great convention . . . nominating the weakest candidate before it. How many of the delegates were honestly for him I don't know, but . . . [t]here was absolutely nothing in his record to make them eager for him." Political commentator Walter Lippmann described Roosevelt contemptuously as "an amiable boy scout."

The choice of John Nance Garner, Speaker of the House, for the second spot on the ticket exacerbated the problem. The popular Texan was much better known and more experienced than Roosevelt. One disappointed Texas colleague complained, "It's a kangaroo ticket. Stronger in the hindquarters than in the front."

With a platform that promised unemployment relief, sweeping programs to put people back to work, stock market regulation, and the repeal of Prohibition, anyone the Democrats ran would almost certainly have been elected in 1932. The embattled Republicans were stuck with Hoover, who insisted on running again.

The president was now so disliked that audiences often booed him when he made public appearances.

The Republicans did their best, attacking Roosevelt as a radical and a socialist. Hoover predicted economic ruin if the Democratic ticket was elected, saying "grass would grow in the streets of one hundred cities." Republicans also questioned whether Roosevelt was healthy enough to be president—polio had left him paralyzed from the waist down since 1921. Roosevelt answered his critics with a vigorous cross-country campaign, giving dozens of speeches in front of cheering crowds. He told them, "My policy is as radical as American liberty, as radical as the Constitution."

Americans were obviously convinced. Nearly 58 percent of voters went for the kangaroo ticket.

Boondoggles

The quirky word *boondoggles* sprang into popularity in the mid-1930s. It originally referred to small, useful items made out of leather or rope, such as belts. The public's attention was drawn to boondoggles with this April 4, 1935, *New York Times* headline: "$3,187,000 Relief Is Spent to Teach Jobless to Play; . . . 'Boon Doggles' Made." The article described a government program that instructed the unemployed in various leisure-time activities.

The exact origins of *boondoggle* are unclear. According to one person interviewed for the *Times* article, it was an old pioneer word for gadgets. A *Chicago Tribune* article from around the same time claimed that the word originated with cowboys, who used it as a name for saddle ornaments made out of leather scraps. Other sources credit Rochester, New York, scoutmaster Robert H. Link with coining or popularizing the word. Among the Boy Scouts, a boondoggle was a braided leather lanyard with a whistle or other object dangling from it.

Once *boondoggle* appeared in connection with relief programs, New Deal opponents snatched it up eagerly as a metaphor for wasteful spending. During the 1936 election campaign, Republicans used the word to label Roosevelt's newly formed government agencies, implying that they were frivolous wastes of time and money. Roosevelt retaliated by calling foreign loans made under the Hoover administration "foreign boondoggles."

In recent decades the meaning of *boondoggle* has shifted slightly. Now it often applies to congressional junkets, hometown pork projects, and similar expenditures of taxpayer money.

Nine Old Men

Roosevelt initiated the New Deal with a blast of legislation. He put people back to work with large-scale projects ranging from dam building to mural painting. He also moved to regulate the banks and exert control over industry. Nearly all his reforms passed easily through Congress, but some programs hit roadblocks when they came before the conservative Supreme Court.

The centerpiece of Roosevelt's plan to restructure business and industry was the National Recovery Act, which set wages, hours, and prices, including restrictions on child labor. The Supreme Court declared the act unconstitutional on the grounds that it regulated businesses at the local level. The Court also threw out the Agricultural Adjustment Act, which restricted the type and amount of crops that farmers could sell.

Roosevelt was furious. He attacked the justices as arrogant old men—they ranged in age from sixty-one to eighty—whose attitudes dated from "the horse and buggy" era. This picture of the Court was reinforced with the 1936 publication of a book titled *The Nine Old Men*. Authored by journalists Drew Pearson and Robert Allen, the book portrayed the Supreme Court as antiquated and reactionary. References to "the nine old men" of the Court began appearing in print.

After winning the 1936 election, Roosevelt announced a plan to "save the Constitution from the Court and the Court from itself." He proposed that if any federal court judge failed to retire by six months after his seventieth birthday, the president could appoint an "assistant judge" to help him do his work. Roosevelt wanted to be allowed to appoint up to six extra judges to the Supreme Court. Obviously they would be New Deal supporters.

Roosevelt's proposal was a misstep. It met with strong resistance, from both the public and Congress. Even Democrats who normally supported the president were cool to the idea. Opponents called the plan "court packing." It was ultimately buried in committee and never came to a vote. Ironically, Supreme Court justices began retiring or dying shortly into Roosevelt's second term. Eventually he was able to appoint seven people to the Court, largely ending the judicial opposition to his programs.

1936

FRANKLIN D. ROOSEVELT (DEMOCRAT) VS. ALFRED LANDON (REPUBLICAN)

That Madman in the White House

For most Americans, the New Deal was all about Roosevelt. Shortly after taking office, he brought the case for his policies directly to the people in a series of folksy radio broadcasts he dubbed "Fireside Chats." Millions of citizens, heartened by this personal touch, were ready to support the New Deal because they loved the president. Roosevelt's personal popularity remained strong throughout his time in office, even among those who didn't entirely support New Deal programs.

The other side of the coin was, in the words of one journalist, the "consuming personal hatred" that obsessed a large section of the upper class. Although taxes had not risen much under the Roosevelt administration and the stock market was climbing, many people were convinced that New Deal policies spelled the end of civilization as the wealthy had known it. They called Roosevelt a traitor to his class. This group hated the president's wife, Eleanor, almost as much as they loathed her husband. A rumor circulated that the Roosevelts were planning to form a dynasty, with Mrs. Roosevelt slated to take over from the president until their sons were ready for the top job.

One common nickname among Roosevelt haters was That Madman in the White House or, more brutally, That Cripple in the White House. Other nicknames included the New Deal Caesar, the Raw Dealocrat, Kangaroosevelt (harking back to the 1932 election), and Franklin Deficit Roosevelt. The noisy demagogue Father Charles Coughlin, a disillusioned former New Dealer, called the president Franklin Double-Crossing Roosevelt when ranting against him over the radio.

As the 1936 election drew near, Republicans focused on the theme of Roosevelt's aggressive governing style. Their platform complained that he had usurped the powers of Congress, attacked the authority and dignity of the Supreme Court, and violated the traditions of free enterprise. They also promised to "stop the folly of uncontrolled spending." The cars of anti–New Dealers sported "Save the Constitution" license plates.

Republican presidential candidate Alf Landon read the following comment on the president's governing style into the *Congressional Record*: "I'm tired, oh so tired, of the whole New Deal / Of the juggler's smile and the barker's spiel / Of the mushy speech and the loud bassoon / And tiredest of all of our leader's croon."

The Republican National Committee launched an attack on the new Social Security Act, set to go into effect in January 1937. They distributed leaflets in industrial areas warning that workers would be "sentenced to a weekly pay reduction" for the rest of their working lives unless they voted for Landon. Businesses helped the cause by slipping notices into their employees' pay envelopes stating, "Effective January, 1937 we are compelled by a Roosevelt 'New Deal' law to make a 1 per cent deduction from your wages and turn it over to the government." (They didn't mention that employers would also be required to cough up 1 percent.)

The Republicans undercut their own message by actually supporting the basics of the New Deal, but claiming that they would run the programs more efficiently and with a balanced budget. Roosevelt ridiculed the notion that they could implement recovery programs without spending money, calling it a "smooth evasion." He also reminded voters that the Republican Party was the party of Hoover. "Who is there in America," he asked, "who believes that we can run the risk of turning back our government to the old leadership which brought it to the brink of 1933?"

Anti-Roosevelt newspapers—and there were many—trotted out familiar charges of communism. Papers owned by William Randolph Hearst were especially hostile to the president, accusing him of being in thrall to Soviet Russia. They printed ditties about "A Red New Deal with a Soviet Seal." Editorials predicted that a Roosevelt victory would mean Soviets running the White House. A typical *Chicago Tribune* headline shouted, "Moscow Orders Reds in U.S. to Back Roosevelt." Mencken called the president "a blood-brother of Lenin" and likened his smile to that of Soviet dictator Joseph Stalin.

Roosevelt made feisty responses to these attacks. He energetically defended the Social Security program, pointing out that most Republicans in Congress had voted for it. He declared that he welcomed the hatred of his attackers: "I should like to have it said of my first administration that in it the forces of selfishness and of lust for power met their match."

In spite of the buckets of mud being thrown at the president, he was able to defeat his opponent handily. Landon was a colorless man who failed to inspire, while Roosevelt continued to move Americans with his Fireside Chats and powerful campaign speeches. Although the country was not yet out of depression, the situation was improving. Most people were satisfied with the New Deal and with the president. Roosevelt's majority was even larger than in 1932—over 60 percent of the vote. He carried every state except Maine and Vermont.

Bleeding Hearts

The first uses of *bleeding heart* to mean "someone tenderhearted toward the downtrodden" began appearing in the 1930s. Before that time the phrase described someone who was suffering emotionally, such as a bereaved person. In its new meaning, it describes people whose hearts bleed sympathetically for others, but with the implication that they are suckers or lack common sense.

The political meaning of *bleeding heart* may have been coined by conservative columnist Westbrook Pegler. It first appeared in print in a January 8, 1938, column in which Pegler criticized a "time-killing debate" on antilynching laws, noting that only around fourteen people a year were lynched. In Pegler's view, the country's other problems were more pressing. He writes, "I question the humanitarianism of any professional or semi-pro bleeding heart who clamors that not a single person must be allowed to hunger, but would stall the entire legislative program . . . to save 14 lives a year."

Bleeding hearts were often connected with the New Deal in the 1930s, as in another Pegler phrase, "bleeding-heart journalists of the New Deal." The negative expression *bleeding heart liberal* didn't come into vogue until the 1960s. *Liberal* on its own didn't become a pejorative term until around the 1980s (see Chapter 8).

1940

FRANKLIN D. ROOSEVELT (DEMOCRAT) VS. WENDELL WILLKIE (REPUBLICAN)

A Third Term or a Third Rater

The 1940 election played out against a background of world-wide turmoil. Nazi Germany under Adolf Hitler had annexed the Rhineland, Austria, and Czechoslovakia and was clearly bent on conquering the rest of western Europe. Fascist Italy had occupied Ethiopia as a start to its own empire. On the other side of the world, imperial Japan overran China and set its sights on Southeast Asia and the Pacific. Americans began to worry that they would be pulled into another foreign war.

Some historians believe that if the European war had not broken out in 1939, Roosevelt would not have run for a third term. As it was, he waited to be "drafted" by the Democratic convention. The president's supporters orchestrated a behind-the-scenes campaign that included stationing one man near a hidden microphone so he could boom out cries of "We want Roosevelt" and "The world needs Roosevelt" at appropriate moments during the speeches. This tactic, along with a dearth of alternative candidates, resulted in Roosevelt's being nominated overwhelmingly on the first ballot.

His opponent was a Wall Street lawyer named Wendell Willkie. Willkie, called by some "the rich man's Roosevelt," had never held a public office. He captured the Republican nomination through a well-organized campaign that relied on a network of booster organizations called Willkie Clubs, as well as frequent public appearances and favorable mentions in the press.

There were few policy differences between the candidates, so Willkie focused on the controversial third-term issue. He accused Roosevelt of thinking himself indispensable and wanting to institute "one-man rule." He habitually referred to the president as "the third-term candidate." Willkie's campaign reignited the fears of those who already believed That Madman was aiming for a dictatorship, even before his decision to run again.

Anti-Roosevelt action committees manufactured millions of lapel buttons with slogans such as "No Franklin the First," "No Royal Family," "We Don't Want Eleanor Either," "Roosevelt for Ex-President," and "No Fourth Term Either." Billboards were erected saying, "Hitler Was Elected the First Three Times" and "Refuse Dictatorship." Roosevelt backers responded with "America Needs Roosevelt," "Two Good Terms Deserve Another," and "Better a Third Term Than a Third Rater."

The other compelling issue of the campaign was the question of whether the United States would enter the war. Roosevelt had recently convinced a reluctant Congress to make wartime loans to England, but a majority of Americans remained determined isolationists. Willkie, who hadn't gotten much traction talking about a third term, started presenting himself as the peace candidate. He told audiences that a vote for Roosevelt meant wooden crosses for their loved ones. He promised that if he were elected president, "no American boys will be sent to the shambles of the European trenches."

Roosevelt felt that he also had to promise to keep the country out of war, except in case of attack. In a speech given in Boston shortly before the election he said, "I have said this before, but I shall say it again and again and again: Your boys are not going to be sent into any foreign wars." He also exaggerated Willkie's commitment to isolationism, remarking, "You can't say that everyone who is opposed to Roosevelt is pro-Nazi, but you *can* say with truth that everyone who is pro-Hitler . . . is pro-Willkie."

Americans were reassured enough by Roosevelt's promises to return him to office, although by the narrowest margin of any of his elections, less than 55 percent. One year later, Roosevelt became a wartime president after all. On December 7, 1941, Japan attacked Pearl Harbor and the United States was plunged into the foreign war it hoped to avoid.

1944

FRANKLIN D. ROOSEVELT (DEMOCRAT) VS. THOMAS E. DEWEY (REPUBLICAN)

The Little Man on the Wedding Cake

In 1944, with the country engulfed in World War II, Democrats took it for granted that Roosevelt would run for a fourth term and he agreed to accept the nomination if the party wanted him. The delegates nominated him on the first ballot. The Republicans selected Thomas E. Dewey, the young first-term governor of New York, who was also chosen almost unanimously on the first ballot.

Dewey was a short, tidy-looking man with black center-parted hair and a toothbrush moustache. He acquired the disparaging nickname of the Little Man on the Wedding Cake. Strangely, the label was apparently invented by a member of his own party. It is most often attributed to Alice Roosevelt Longworth, Theodore Roosevelt's daughter. (Longworth was a lifelong Republican. She didn't like her distant cousin Franklin and didn't vote for him.)

According to a July 10, 1944, *Time* article reporting on the Republican convention, "Alice Longworth . . . gave currency to the *mot* of the Convention: 'How can you vote for a man who looks like the bridegroom on a wedding cake?'" Longworth later told columnist William Safire that she did not coin the phrase. In a letter answering his query she explained that she first heard it from another woman at the convention. She wrote, "I thought it frightfully funny and quoted it to everyone. Then it began to be attributed to me."

Dewey's manner reinforced this unflattering image. He had a fussy speaking style, using exclamations like *good gracious*. He sometimes ended a sentence by saying, "period." He was also stiff and unfriendly with newsmen, many of whom repeated the wedding cake comment to his detriment. It's doubtful whether looking like a miniature bridegroom was a major factor in Dewey's failure to get elected, but the assault on his dignity surely had some negative effect.

Tired Old Men

Dewey's main campaign issue was the obvious one that the Democrats had been in office long enough. Roosevelt, who had earlier labeled the Supreme Court justices as worn-out old men, was now being smeared with the same criticism. In his acceptance speech at the Republican convention, Dewey admitted that the Roosevelt administration had done some good things in its young days. Now, however, "it has grown old in office. It has become tired and quarrelsome." He told the audience that he was concerned that the Democrats were too worn out to achieve a successful peace.

Later that month at the Democratic convention, keynote speaker Governor Robert Kerr of Oklahoma faced the charges head-on. He thundered, "Shall we discard as a tired old man 59-year-old Admiral Nimitz . . . 62-year-old Admiral Halsey . . . 61-year-old General MacArthur? . . . [W]e know we are winning this war with these 'tired old men,' including 62-year-old Roosevelt as their commander-in-chief." The response of Harold Ickes, secretary of the interior, was more devastating. He observed during a speech that the forty-two-year-old Dewey had "thrown his diaper into the ring."

Clear Everything with Sidney

Although Roosevelt was renominated easily, the convention struggled with their choice for vice president. Henry Wallace, who had replaced John Nance Garner as Roosevelt's running mate in 1940, was too far to the left for some sections of the Democratic Party.

For the sake of party unity, Roosevelt agreed to replace him on the ticket. His next choice was adviser James F. Byrnes of South Carolina, but he was too conservative on race and labor issues. Labor leaders such as Sidney Hillman, chairman of the Congress of Industrial Organizations (CIO) Political Action Committee, deemed him absolutely unacceptable.

Roosevelt next chose Missouri senator Harry Truman, who was nominated after two rounds of voting. He became known as "the new Missouri Compromise." According to a story that later appeared in various newspapers and magazines, the president spoke with Bob Hannegan, Democratic national chairman, just before the nominating began. He was supposed to have said, "Go on down there and nominate Truman before there's any more trouble. And clear everything with Sidney," meaning Sidney Hillman.

Hannegan labeled the story "an unmitigated lie." Nonetheless, the Republican campaign embraced this opportunity to sink the president with his own words. They reportedly spent $1 million on radio time to trumpet the phrase "Clear everything with Sidney." In the words of a September 25, 1944, *Time* article, they hoped it would "turn out to be as telling as 'Rum, Romanism, and Rebellion' proved to be in 1884." They told voters, "It's your country—why let Sidney Hillman run it?" They linked Hillman with the Communist Party, which was supporting Roosevelt because he accepted the Russians as wartime allies. The old charges about Roosevelt's communist sympathies were given another airing.

Still, the phrase never packed the same negative punch as the "Rum, Romanism, and Rebellion" cry that finished off James G. Blaine (see Chapter 3). No matter how most Americans felt about communism, they were unwilling to take a chance on a new administration in the middle of a war. Once again, the Democratic ticket won by a comfortable margin.

Gobbledygook

This word for abstruse, long-winded verbiage was coined in 1944 by Maury Maverick, a former Texas congressman then working for the War Production Board. Maverick issued a memo that year urging his colleagues, "Stay off the gobbledygook language. It only fouls people up." Maverick later explained that he had a pompous old turkey gobbler in mind when the nonsense word occurred to him. He further defined the word in a *New York Times Magazine* article for May 21, 1944: "talk or writing which is long, pompous, vague, involved, usually with Latinized words."

Gobbledygook soon became the preferred label for the talk of government bureaucrats, as well as a highly popular way for politicians to describe the views of their opponents. The word has stayed in favor over the decades. It is still heard frequently in congressional speeches and appears in hundreds of op-ed pieces every year.

Fellow Travelers

A second Red Scare swept the United States in the 1940s, fueled partly by fears that Soviet spies would steal America's nuclear secrets. *Fellow traveler* (also spelled *traveller*), meaning "a communist sympathizer," gained currency around this time. The term may have been invented by Leon Trotsky, who discussed "literary fellow-travellers" in his 1924 book *Literature and Revolution*. Trotsky was referring to Russian writers who supported the aims of the revolution, but did not write specifically communist literature.

At first *fellow traveler* encompassed those who sympathized with any political cause. *The Nation* for October 24, 1936, describes it this way: "The new phenomenon is the fellow-traveler. [It] means someone who does not accept all your aims but has enough in common with you to accompany you in a comradely fashion part of the way." During the late 1940s and 1950s, as anticommunist hysteria reached its peak, the term became a way of attacking anyone with even vaguely left political views (see Chapter 6 for related terms).

Fellow traveler is still used to describe communist sympathizers. However, it can once again mean someone in tune with any political ideology. The *Christian Science Monitor* for November 5, 2009, for example, contains the line: "He is not at all an ideological fellow traveler of conservative Doug Hoffman, the candidate in New York's 23rd Congressional District."

Coat-Holders and Cookie Pushers

Coat-holders were the 1940s version of ward heelers—political followers who held the big guy's coat while he did the actual fighting. One early use comes from the *Salisbury Times* of Maryland for November 11, 1941, about a month before the attack on Pearl Harbor catapulted the country into war. In an article describing a congressional decision to allow American ships to travel freely in the Atlantic, the *Times* says, "When a nation arms its vessels and then sends them where the shooting is going on . . . we have dropped the last vestige of our attitude as a coat-holder and will be in the battle without pretense."

The *Times* quotation uses *coat-holder* to mean "a supporter"—in this case, of England—but usually the word implies a gofer. The term is still current, as in this example from the *New York Post-Standard* for September 8, 2002: "Cuomo called [Governor Pataki] Giuliani's coat holder in the days after Sept. 11."

Cookie pushers got no more respect than coat-holders. According to the *Saturday Review of Literature* for July 24, 1943, "'Cookie pushers' is a newspaper men's term for thwarted 'career' men in the State Dept. . . . who wear striped trousers and know the proper gambits for unattractive wives of foreign secretaries." In other words, cookie pushers were minor diplomats who wasted their days socializing while their more serious colleagues engaged in the actual work of foreign affairs.

Cookie pusher was originally slang for a young college man who spent his time lounging around with young women at tea parties and the like. A synonym was *tea hound*. The term may have received its political meaning from Hugh Gibson, minister to Finland in the 1920s. A *Washington Post* story for January 18, 1924, describes Gibson as an advocate of "chasing the tea hounds and cookie pushers out of the diplomatic service." Democratic congressman John J. Rooney popularized the label in the 1940s. Representative Rooney, who chaired the subcommittee in charge of State Department appropriations, kept on the lookout for cookie pushers and other money wasters.

Cookie pusher was a familiar term in political circles at least until 1989. That year, a participant on the CNN program *Capital Gang* referred derisively to "the striped-pants cookie pushers in the State Department."

1948

HARRY TRUMAN (DEMOCRAT) VS.
THOMAS E. DEWEY (REPUBLICAN)

Stirring Up the Animals

In 1948 Thomas Dewey again ran for president. This time his opponent was Harry Truman, who stepped into the presidency when Franklin Roosevelt died on April 12, 1945. Truman successfully guided the United States through the final months of the war. However, he stumbled when shepherding the country into the postwar era. His policies drew criticism from both left and right. A 1946 *Life* article titled "A Year of Truman" rounded up current Truman insults—"To err is Truman," "delirium Trumans," "I'm just mild about Harry," and "a sedative in a blue serge suit."

The Republicans were confident that, after sixteen years of Democratic rule, 1948 belonged to them. Truman's approval rating at the beginning of election season was only 50 percent. To make matters worse for the Democrats, southern conservatives were running South Carolina senator Strom Thurmond on the States' Rights ("Dixiecrat") ticket, and the Progressive Party was running former vice president Henry Wallace. Both were sure to draw votes away from the president.

The Republicans' plan was to sit tight. They had no wish to start pointless controversies when they believed that Truman was bound to lose the election anyway. Dewey's press secretary, James Hagerty, later explained their campaign strategy this way: "The main campaign worry was not to rock the boat. . . . State chairmen and local leaders . . . kept saying, telegraphing, and writing that the campaign had to be kept on a low level, that there was no need to stir up the animals."

Truman thought otherwise. He breezily told convention delegates during his acceptance speech, "Senator Barkley [the vice presidential candidate] and I will win this election and make these Republicans like it." He promised to fight hard and "give 'em hell." Truman crisscrossed the country by train, drawing crowds at every stop. People enjoyed his friendly, colloquial manner. He introduced his wife, Bess, as "the boss." He gave rousing speeches against the Republican-dominated "do nothing" Congress and "the bunch of old mossbacks" running the Republican Party.

His energy contrasted strikingly with his opponent's stiffness. Dewey was still the man on the wedding cake to many people. Richard Rovere of the *New Yorker* commented that Dewey came out onstage "like a man who has been mounted on casters and given a tremendous shove from behind." Nor did he have anything new to offer in the way of policy. His speeches were mostly a rehash of his 1944 promises to run the country more efficiently.

The worst negativity that Truman endured was the universal assumption that Dewey would soon be president. Every poll showed Truman lagging behind, usually by several points. The newspapers unanimously predicted Truman's defeat. As the *New York Sun* put it on October 4, "The main question is whether Governor Dewey will win by a fair margin or by a landslide." *Life* published a photograph of Dewey with the caption "The next President of the United States." The *Chicago Tribune* felt confident enough of the election's outcome to send out the next day's early edition with the headline "Dewey Defeats Truman."

They all were wrong. Truman defeated Dewey with a plurality of the popular vote and a large majority of the electoral vote. After the election, the triumphant president was photographed holding a copy of the *Tribune* with its famously mistaken headline.

Pollsters and the press engaged in a lengthy postmortem that included much hand-wringing and groveling. Several explanations were proposed for the wide gap between the experts' perceptions and the election's reality. Polling was "an infant science" subject to statistical errors. Newspapermen had relied too much on the polls and not done enough interviewing. The two minor party candidates, Wallace and Thurmond, failed to draw the expected number of votes away from the Democrats. Dewey himself suggested that a few million overconfident Republican voters may have stayed at home. In fact, if Dewey had not been so careful to avoid stirring up the animals, he might have inspired more of them to get out and vote for him.

With the 1948 election, the Roosevelt era was definitely over. No similar era would ever again be possible. In 1947, Congress passed the Twenty-Second Amendment to the Constitution, limiting future presidents to two terms plus two years in office.

★ **6** ★

Peaceniks

POSTWAR AMERICA AND THE 1960S

1952–1968

A fter World War II ended, Americans focused on domestic politics. Long-standing fears of communist infiltration now reached fever pitch, inflamed by the realization that the Soviets had the Bomb. With Wisconsin senator Joseph McCarthy leading the hunt for card-carrying commies, red baiting became the campaign tactic of choice. Any sign that a political hopeful was soft on America's erstwhile ally the Soviet Union spelled trouble for his candidacy.

Campaigning in the 1950s took on an added dimension as candidates began appearing on television for the first time. Those like Dwight D. Eisenhower who mastered the thirty-second advertising spot held a distinct advantage. A telegenic candidate such as John F. Kennedy could undermine his less fortunate opponent simply by appearing more presidential on the small screen.

During the 1960s, mudslinging took to the streets. Antiwar marches turned into shouting matches between participants and bystanders. Political rallies drew hecklers who traded insults with the speakers onstage. The era's political fury peaked at the 1968 Democratic nominating convention. Vehemently opposed wings of the party attacked each other verbally while, outside the convention hall, Chicago police used billy clubs to control hordes of protesters.

1952

DWIGHT D. EISENHOWER (REPUBLICAN) VS. ADLAI STEVENSON (DEMOCRAT)

The Extremely General Eisenhower Trounces Adlai the Appeaser

For the 1952 election, the Republicans took the traditional route of choosing a war hero for their candidate—former general Dwight D. Eisenhower, affectionately known to millions of Americans as Ike. The Democratic nominee was Adlai Stevenson, chosen when Truman announced that he would not run again. Stevenson had been planning to run for governor of Illinois, but after his powerful convention speech fellow party members convinced him to run for president instead.

The Republican campaign slogan was "K_1C_2"—Korea, Communism, and Corruption. They didn't get very far with corruption. Eisenhower promised to "clean up the mess" brought about by runaway big government, but at the same time he embraced the Democrats' basic New Deal programs, as previous Republican candidates had done.

Eisenhower's early speeches were so bland that reporters nicknamed him the Extremely General Eisenhower. According to one widely circulated story, a newspaperman on the Republican campaign train asked, "Where are we now?" Sighed his companion, "Crossing the thirty-eighth platitude." (Thirty-eight degrees latitude, the boundary between North and South Korea, was on everyone's mind at the time.) The Scripps-Howard newspapers, which supported Eisenhower, complained that he was "running like a dry creek."

Nor was Adlai Stevenson as scintillating as expected. Although a compelling speaker during live appearances, he was unable to adjust to the new medium of television. His campaign purchased thirty-minute blocks of time, during which Stevenson stood alone in front of the camera delivering dense policy speeches. Often he ran overtime and the penny-conscious networks cut him off in midsentence. Eisenhower's managers understood the potential of the small screen much better. His campaign gained traction when the Republicans ran a series of brisk thirty-second spots titled "Eisenhower Answers the Nation."

Eisenhower gained the biggest advantage by focusing on the communist threat. He called the Democratic platform "un-American" and promised to purge the country's institutions of "the subversive and the disloyal" who had "poisoned two whole decades of our national life." He criticized those who did not have "the sense or the stamina" to fight communism at home.

Eisenhower thoroughly disliked Senator Joseph McCarthy but allowed himself to be maneuvered into endorsing McCarthy's run for reelection. Many Eisenhower supporters were disappointed by what they saw as his surrender to the right wing of the party, and Stevenson's criticism was scathing. He accused his opponent of embracing policies he didn't believe in just to get elected, saying during a rally that Eisenhower was "waging a crusade to make the world safe for hypocrisy."

Eisenhower's running mate Richard Nixon was a tireless slinger of anticommunist mud. He referred to Stevenson as "Adlai the Appeaser" and "a Ph.D. graduate of [Secretary of State] Dean Acheson's Cowardly College of Communist Containment." Nixon accused the Truman administration of allowing "the godless Red Tide to . . . engulf millions" and told voters that both Russian and American communists wanted a Democratic victory in November.

Stevenson responded to these accusations by attacking his opponents' bullying methods. He told an audience at the University of Wisconsin, "[W]e are . . . fighting those who, in the name of anti-communism, would assail the community of freedom itself. . . . I should shudder for this country if I thought that we, too, must surrender to the sinister figure of the inquisition." Taking a dig at McCarthy, he also said, "Catching real Communist agents, like killing poisonous snakes or tigers, is not a job for amateurs or children, especially noisy ones."

What finally put Eisenhower over the top was an early version of a tactic later known as an "October surprise"—springing a negative surprise on an opponent late in the campaign (see Chapter 7). While giving a speech in Detroit on October 24, Eisenhower promised that ending the stalemated Korean War would be a top priority. His first move would be to investigate the situation for himself. He said, "Only in that way could I learn how best to serve the American people in the cause of peace. I shall go to Korea."

This announcement caused a sensation. Democrats accused Eisenhower of grandstanding, but voters were thrilled. Eisenhower buried Stevenson at the polls, with 442 electoral votes to Stevenson's 89.

Eggheads

Adlai Stevenson was an articulate man who gave information-packed speeches. He gained the reputation of being an intellectual, or as his Republican opponents contemptuously put it, an "egghead." The word had been around since the early twentieth century. It suggests that people with extra-large brains have high-domed, egg-shaped foreheads.

New York Herald Tribune columnist Stewart Alsop first applied the term to Stevenson. In his September 27, 1952, column, Alsop described a conversation he had while attending a Stevenson speech on atomic energy. He had remarked to "a rising young Connecticut Republican" sitting near him that many intelligent people who usually voted Republican seemed to admire Stevenson. The reply was, "Sure, all the egg-heads love Stevenson. But how many egg-heads do you think there are?" Alsop then posed the question, "How many people, not egg-heads themselves, admire and would vote for such an obvious 'egg-head' as Adlai Stevenson?" The implied answer is, "not many."

Stevenson joked about the nickname, declaiming during one speech, "Eggheads of the world unite; you have nothing to lose but your yolks!" Nonetheless, his perceived eggheadedness was a problem for his campaign, especially contrasted with Ike's relaxed "everyman" style. Although Eisenhower complained that his campaign managers presented him as someone who didn't have a brain in his head, the voters obviously preferred his short, upbeat remarks over Stevenson's lengthy disquisitions.

During the 1950s and 1960s *egghead* was a common putdown of the intellectually or culturally serious, a slangier version of *highbrow*. The word is not as popular now as it was in Stevenson's day, but it still occasionally appears in print.

The Dinosaur Wing

In a Salt Lake City speech given on October 14, Stevenson assigned the label *dinosaur wing* to the most conservative section of the Republican Party. He spoke of "Republicans (the dinosaur wing of that party) . . . who call everything 'creeping socialism.'" He may have been inspired by a *New York Times* article of the day before in which a member of the Democratic Party was quoted as saying that Republicans who complained about cronyism in the Truman administration were "hypocritical old dinosaurs."

Earlier that year Truman himself had made a speech characterizing Republicans as economically backward-looking because they did not support strategies to keep wages and farm prices high. He declared that Republicans were controlled by "the dinosaur wing" of the party, whose "hearts lie with the corporations and not with the working people." He also suggested that their opposition to intervention in Korea stemmed from a dinosaur-like isolationism.

Since the 1950s, *dinosaur wing* has been used to characterize reactionaries or entrenched old-timers of either party.

Card-Carrying Commies, Commie Symps, and Reds Under the Bed

As World War II ended, the United States and the Soviet Union began what is known as the Cold War—a struggle for political dominance of the postwar world. When the Soviets tested their first atomic bomb in 1949, Americans started to worry about the possibility of nuclear Armageddon. Many became obsessed with the idea that communists in the United States would pass atomic secrets to the Russians, giving them a competitive edge.

The House Un-American Activities Committee began investigating hundreds of people they suspected of communist leanings. Although most had little or no connection with the Communist Party, the country was suddenly abuzz with concern over card-carrying commies.

A typical headline comes from Iowa's *Cedar Rapids Gazette* for February 19, 1950: "54,000 Card-Carrying Commies in U.S." Until this time, *card-carrying* simply meant someone who held a membership card for a labor union or other organization, but in the 1950s the phrase was usually followed by *communist*.

Of more concern than card-carrying commies were sympathizers who kept quiet about their views. The 1940s term for such people was *fellow travelers*. In the 1950s, they were called *commie symps*. The original term was *ComSymp*, invented by Robert Welch Jr., founder of the anticommunist John Birch Society. *Commie symp* was more common, probably because *commie* had been part of the vocabulary since the 1920s. Unlike party members, commie symps could lurk in government offices, schools, or other workplaces with no one the wiser.

Fears of hidden communists led to frantic searches for reds under the bed. This expression began appearing during the 1930s, but is most often associated with the 1950s. The phrase was widely used, both by critics of anticommunist witch hunts and those in favor of them. For instance, an August 23, 1952, editorial in the *Mason City (IA) Globe-Gazette* comments, "Seeing Reds under every bed certainly is not as bad as the opposite assumption, namely, that there is no communist problem."

McCarthyism

Joseph McCarthy, an obscure first-term senator from Wisconsin, took advantage of anticommunist fever to give his own career a spectacular boost. McCarthy shot to fame in 1950 when he announced during a Lincoln Day speech in Wheeling, West Virginia, that he had a list of 205 communists employed by the State Department. Although his claim was later shown to be false, he went on to mount a zealous campaign against potential communist traitors in the government.

McCarthy used his position as chair of the Senate Committee on Government Operations to investigate such agencies as the

Red terms have died out since the collapse of the Soviet Union in 1991. *Card-carrying* is still used, often humorously, to designate someone strongly identified with a particular group or set of ideas. It frequently appears in connection with political terms, such as *card-carrying liberal*, but it can identify any kind of group. A 2007 *Syracuse Post-Standard* review of novels based on the *Star Trek* television series mentions "card carrying Trekkers and Trekkies."

Voice of America and the International Information Agency for communist infiltration. Rather than producing hard evidence, he relied on scurrilous innuendoes and personal invective to take down his victims.

Political cartoonist Herbert Block, who signed his drawings Herblock, popularized *McCarthyism* to describe these tactics. He first used the term in a cartoon that appeared in the *Washington Post* on March 29, 1950, depicting a resistant GOP elephant being pushed to stand on top of a wobbly platform of mud buckets, the top one of which is labeled "McCarthyism." (Although Block is often credited with inventing the term, it was apparently in circulation earlier. For instance, it appears in a March 28, 1950, editorial in the *Christian Science Monitor*.)

McCarthy overreached when he conducted an investigation of the U.S. Army. The army retaliated by bringing corruption charges against McCarthy. Televised hearings of the case exposed

McCarthy as a blustering bully, and he lost most of his popular support. Soon thereafter, the Senate censured his behavior, effectively ending his political career. He died in 1957.

Since McCarthy's day, the term *McCarthyism* has expanded to cover any sort of accusations that rely on smear tactics rather than due process. For instance, beginning in the 1980s, *sexual McCarthyism* has been used to label attacks based on someone's sexual behavior or orientation.

1956

DWIGHT D. EISENHOWER (REPUBLICAN) VS. ADLAI STEVENSON (DEMOCRAT)

Eisenhower and Stevenson faced off again in 1956. Stevenson's chances of victory were even slimmer this time around. Eisenhower remained tremendously popular in spite of a recent heart attack that had some wondering whether he would be physically up to another term.

In fact, Eisenhower was so sure of winning that he did little campaigning. Stevenson, in contrast, traveled around the country pitching his "New America" platform—proposed social programs such as medical insurance for senior citizens, combined with a call to ban nuclear weapons testing. He gained little traction with these ideas. Most Americans still "liked Ike," as the Eisenhower campaign buttons put it. He won a landslide victory, taking 457 electoral votes to Stevenson's 73.

1960

John F. Kennedy (Democrat) vs. Richard Nixon (Republican)

Tricky Dick and the Brash Young Man

In 1960 the Democrats nominated Massachusetts senator John F. Kennedy for president. If elected, he would be the youngest man ever to hold that office. Kennedy was handsome and charismatic, with a well-oiled campaign machine. His main weakness as a candidate was his youth. The Republicans (and many old-school Democrats) considered him a "brash young man," lacking in the experience necessary to run the country.

His Republican opponent, Richard M. Nixon, finishing his second term as Eisenhower's vice president, ran on the slogan "Experience counts." Kennedy responded by using Nixon's incumbency against him. "Mr. Nixon is experienced," he said, "experienced in policies of retreat, defeat, and weakness." He emphasized the current administration's failure to compete effectively against the Russians, especially in the matter of sending satellites comparable to the Soviet *Sputnik* into outer space.

The Kennedy campaign resurrected the *Tricky Dick* label first used by California Democrats during Nixon's 1950 senatorial run.

To counter a Nixon ad that attempted to persuade Democratic voters that he was one of them, the California Democratic committee had run a full-page newspaper ad calling attention to "'Tricky Dick' Nixon's Republican record." Now the catchy nickname was put into national circulation. Posters also appeared with a picture of a glowering Nixon and the caption "Would you buy a used car from this man?"

Besides his youth, Kennedy's other problem was his Catholicism. Nixon refused to campaign on this issue, but abusive anti-Catholic pamphlets nonetheless circulated widely. Hostile signs saying, "We don't want the Kremlin or the Vatican" appeared at Kennedy rallies. More seriously, an organization of Protestant ministers headed by the prominent author Dr. Norman Vincent Peale published a statement expressing concern that a Catholic president would be under pressure to "bring American foreign policy into line with Vatican objectives."

Kennedy combated the issue by insisting repeatedly that he believed in the absolute separation of church and state and pointing out that, as a senator, he had already taken an oath of loyalty to the Constitution. Perhaps more effectively, Democratic vice presidential candidate Lyndon Johnson gave what he termed his "little ole war hero speech," reminding audiences that when Kennedy's brother Joe and other World War II heroes died for their country, no one asked about their religion. Anti-Catholic feeling was not as strong as it had been in Al Smith's day and the issue eventually faded. It has not reappeared as a central issue in any presidential campaign since 1960.

Both candidates suffered through negative comments from

members of their own party. Before the Democratic convention, Eleanor Roosevelt remarked during a television interview that Kennedy was "a charming young man" whose father was spending "oodles of money" to get him elected. Kennedy challenged her publicly to give an example of such spending. Mrs. Roosevelt eventually admitted that she did not know of a specific case. However, she remained extremely reluctant to endorse Kennedy after he was nominated.

Nixon's difficulties sprang from Eisenhower's unwillingness to give him credit for the experience that he claimed as vice president. Asked during one press conference to give an example of a major idea that Nixon had contributed during his two terms, Eisenhower snapped, "If you give me a week, I might think of one." The Democrats made the most of this unscripted comment.

Nixon's worst enemy turned out to be the television camera. In a historic step, Nixon and Kennedy agreed to four televised debates. For the first time, millions of voters would be able to view the candidates in action. The first debate, broadcast from Chicago on September 26, 1960, has served ever since as a cautionary tale for presidential hopefuls.

The difference in style between the two candidates was striking. Kennedy, looking tanned, fit, and relaxed, spoke directly to the television audience. Rather than enmeshing himself in fine points of policy, he spoke in broad terms, offering an upbeat vision for America's future. At the same time, he produced enough facts and details to impress those worried about his lack of governing experience.

Nixon, in contrast, looked haggard, sweaty, and disheveled.

He was recovering from a badly infected knee, which had put him in the hospital and caused him to lose weight. His five o'clock shadow showed through streaks of a product called Lazy Shave, inexpertly applied by his staffers. After the event, his mother called to ask if he was ill. Chicago mayor Richard Daley was heard to exclaim, "They've embalmed him before he even died," and the next day several newspapers noted that he looked unwell. Nixon also made a poor impression as a debater. He focused on refuting small points in Kennedy's statements, addressing his arguments to the moderators rather than the folks at home.

Although people listening to the radio were evenly divided over who won, television viewers named Kennedy by a wide margin. The two men were better matched during subsequent debates, but Nixon never recovered from the disaster of his first appearance. Kennedy's greater on-screen appeal gave him the boost he needed to win an extremely close election.

Hatchet Men

This slang term for political enforcers, although not new, started to become more common during the 1960s. It is probably an allusion to the colonial army's hatchet men. These were men who went ahead of the soldiers and cleared a path by chopping away the undergrowth. Political hatchet men clear the way for the candidate by strong-arming supporters and slinging mud at opponents. They do the dirty work so the person running for office can concentrate on appealing to the voters.

During the 1960 presidential campaign, both candidates were known to employ hatchet men. The British *News-Chronicle*, describing the Democratic convention, told readers, "The Kennedy family went into action with a commando team of political hatchet-men." Toward the end of the campaign, the *Daily Telegram* of Columbus, Nebraska, wrote about Republicans distributing leaflets throughout traditionally Democratic Nebraska towns. Commented one observer, "Nixon's hatchet men always live in hope that they can find a few strays."

Hatchet men (and women) still exist in abundance. Many these days have their own blogs or other public outlets.

1964

LYNDON B. JOHNSON (DEMOCRAT) VS. BARRY GOLDWATER (REPUBLICAN)

In Your Guts, You Know He's Nuts

Barry Goldwater, the 1964 Republican nominee for president, took some heavy bashing. His critics included moderate Republicans disturbed by his militant attitude toward the Soviet Union and his ferocious opposition to social programs. Worse, the Arizona senator was known for his maladroit off-the-cuff remarks. He worried publicly about the reliability of Defense Department missiles. He expressed a desire to lob an atomic bomb into the men's room of the Kremlin. He commented during a news conference that the country might be better off if "we could just saw off the Eastern Seaboard and let it float out to sea."

New York governor Nelson Rockefeller, the candidate of choice for the Republican center, considered Goldwater and his supporters "kooks." Conservative *New Republic* editor Walter Lippmann wrote, "Barry Goldwater is not a conservative at all . . . he is a radical reactionary who would, if we are to believe what he says, dismantle the modern state." However, Goldwater was popular with the grass roots. He had the support of most delegates at the Republican convention and was quickly nominated.

The moderates' worst fears were realized when they heard Goldwater's fire-breathing acceptance speech. Loosely quoting Cicero, he uttered a line that became instantly notorious: "Extremism in the defense of liberty is no vice!" Shouted one stunned reporter, "My God! He's going to run as Barry Goldwater."

The Democratic candidate was Lyndon Johnson, who became president when John Kennedy was assassinated in November 1963. President Johnson left the early campaigning to his supporters. These included a group of White House insiders calling themselves "the Five O'Clock Club," who met after work hours to develop ideas for smearing their opponent. One Democratic tactic was to portray Goldwater as a dangerous radical eager to deploy nuclear weapons. They called him Dr. Strangewater, an allusion to the 1964 movie *Dr. Strangelove*, a satire about a crazed air force general who orders a nuclear attack against the Soviet Union.

They also ran a television ad that became known as "the Daisy Ad." It features a little girl counting the petals of a daisy-like flower. As she reaches "nine," a man's voice starts counting down. The camera zooms in on the girl's eye until her pupil fills the screen. When the voice says, "zero," viewers see a flash of light and a mushroom cloud reflected in her vision. "The Daisy Ad" aired only once, but made an indelible impact on millions of voters.

In response to the Republican slogan "In your heart, you know he's right," Democrats said, "Yes—extreme right." They parodied the slogan with "In your heart, you know he might" (explode an atom bomb) and "In your guts, you know he's nuts." In an echo of the 1896 campaign against William Jennings Bryan, *Fact* magazine polled over twelve thousand psychiatrists, asking whether Goldwater was psychologically fit to be president. Of the approximately twenty-four hundred who replied, well over half answered no. Both the American Psychiatric Association and the American Medical Association criticized the unscientific poll. Still, it had an effect.

The Democrats also used Goldwater's own past statements against him. Arthur Frommer compiled a collection of Goldwater quotations in a 115-page book titled *Goldwater from A to Z*. The book provided much useful attack fodder, such as Goldwater's rueful admission during an interview, "You know, I haven't got a really first-class brain."

Republicans fought back by portraying Johnson as an ambitious wheeler-dealer who associated with corporate criminals. They pointed to his long friendship with entrepreneur Robert G. "Bobby" Baker, then under Senate investigation. They accused Johnson of building a private fortune by dubious means. Goldwater warned that, to Johnson, the presidency meant "craving and grasping for power—more and more and more, without end."

Republicans also played up Johnson's "corn-pone" persona—his coarse language, his habit of lifting his beagles by their ears, and the way he sped around his ranch in his Lincoln Continental while tossing back cans of beer. Goldwater drew the line at a twenty-eight-minute film titled *Choice*. The film juxtaposed images of young, clean-cut white conservatives with stripteasers, pornographic book covers, young women in topless swimsuits, and young black urban rioters. These scenes were intercut with glimpses of a speeding Lincoln sedan not unlike LBJ's. The implied choice was between a law-abiding Republican country and the societal collapse brought about by Johnson's domestic policies.

Calling the film racist, Goldwater refused to let it be aired. Even without it, the Republicans succeeded in persuading many Americans that Johnson was responsible for the country's moral decay and rising crime rate.

As Election Day neared, it became apparent that large numbers of people who felt distaste for Johnson were nonetheless preparing to vote for him. Goldwater's aggressive position on communism, especially in Vietnam, scared many voters. Johnson established himself as the peace candidate who preferred negotiation over widening the conflict. Johnson won all but six states—Goldwater's home state of Arizona and five southern states—and garnered a mountain of electoral votes—486 to Goldwater's 52. It was the biggest landslide since Roosevelt beat Alf Landon in 1936.

The Credibility Gap

As the military buildup in Vietnam increased, Americans began to suspect that President Johnson was not telling them the whole truth about the conflict, especially about numbers of casualties. The name given to this growing mistrust was *the credibility gap*.

The term may have appeared first in a *New York Herald Tribune* headline of May 23, 1965: "Dilemma in 'Credibility Gap.'" A *Washington Post* article for December 5 of that year explained the credibility gap phenomenon: "It represents a perceptibly growing disquiet, misgiving or skepticism about the candor or validity of official declarations." Soldiers serving in Vietnam wore buttons that said, "Ambushed at credibility gap."

Anger over developments in Vietnam soon spilled into other areas as well. The credibility gap burgeoned into a general unwillingness to accept administration pronouncements at face value.

Credibility gap has remained in the vocabulary. During the early twenty-first century, it was joined by *truth deficit* (see Chapter 8).

1968

RICHARD NIXON (REPUBLICAN) VS. HUBERT HUMPHREY (DEMOCRAT) VS. GEORGE WALLACE (AMERICAN INDEPENDENT)

Dump the Hump

In a reversal of the usual situation, the challenger in the 1968 presidential campaign had a much smoother run than the incumbent. After a surprisingly strong showing in the Republican primaries, former has-been Richard Nixon easily captured his party's nomination. In contrast, the Democrats were in disarray. Lyndon Johnson was eligible to run again, but as the Vietnam conflict escalated, his popularity plummeted. Opponents of the war began marching in protest, chanting, "Hey, hey, LBJ / How many kids did you kill today?" and "Shut the door on the war / We don't want the draft."

With his support on the decline, Johnson announced in March that he would not seek another term. Several contenders vied to take over the top spot on the Democratic ticket. Minnesota senator Eugene McCarthy did well in the early primaries with an uncompromising stand against the war. Senator Robert Kennedy, the late president's brother, also gathered a following.

The most obvious successor to Johnson was his vice president, Hubert Humphrey. However, as part of the Johnson administration, Humphrey was unpopular with antiwar Democrats. Hecklers attended his campaign speeches and shouted hostile slogans, such as "Dump the Hump," "Don't Hump on me," and "Why change the ventriloquist for the dummy?" Some cried angrily, "Wash the blood off your hands!"

Humphrey struggled to respond effectively to these attacks, but he couldn't distance himself from current Vietnam policies without undercutting the president. To add to his problems, the public began to view his campaign rallies as rowdy events that attracted troublemakers.

By the time the Democratic convention opened in late August, the party was in turmoil. Robert Kennedy had been assassinated in June after winning the California primary, leaving the Democrats deeply shaken. Moreover, the delegates were split into obdurate factions of hawks and doves. Although the McCarthy campaign had lost momentum over the summer, his supporters formed a strong antiwar contingent. Other party members agreed with Humphrey, who was still unwilling to come out openly against the president's handling of the war.

Humphrey, the clear frontrunner, eventually captured the nomination on the first round of voting. However, hawkish and dovish delegates clashed every step of the way, with repeated procedural fights and angry walkouts before the voting finally took place.

The worst struggle occurred over the Vietnam plank of the platform. McCarthy supporters pushed for an unconditional end to the bombing of North Vietnam and a negotiated withdrawal. Johnson, directing activities from the White House, insisted instead on a statement that supported his policies—a halt to the bombing only "when this action would not endanger the lives of our troops" and no unilateral withdrawal. When Johnson's version of the platform was adopted, delegates in the opposition camp donned black armbands and began to sing the civil rights anthem "We Shall Overcome."

Meanwhile, even worse chaos was brewing outside the convention hall. Thousands of antiwar protesters from around the country converged on Chicago with plans to demonstrate. In response, Mayor Daley mobilized twelve thousand police and six thousand National Guard troops. On the third day of the convention, violence broke out. The police waded into a mass of protesters, billy-clubbing anyone within reach, including reporters and other bystanders. Demonstrators reacted by screaming insults and throwing food and rocks. The streets soon turned into a welter of blood and shattered glass. Tear gas hung in the air.

As the tumultuous scene began appearing on television screens around the convention hall, the nominating process temporarily halted while stunned delegates watched the unfolding disaster. Senator Abraham Ribicoff of Connecticut, who was speaking at the time, decried the "Gestapo tactics in the streets of Chicago" to loud applause. Mayor Daley, sitting only yards away, shouted a crude epithet at him. Ribicoff replied, "How hard it is to accept the truth!"

The riot outside the hall added yet more discord to an event already in shambles. The next day, the mayor brought his own supporters to the convention, where they interrupted the proceedings with shouts of "We love Mayor Daley!" Some of the delegates drowned them out by singing "The Battle Hymn of the Republic."

Under these circumstances, it's not surprising that Nixon started the campaign season ahead of Humphrey and stayed ahead. Humphrey gamely challenged Nixon to a debate. When Nixon refused, Humphrey ridiculed him as Sir Richard the Chicken-Hearted and Sir Richard the Unready. He also sneered at Nixon's strong law-and-order stance, calling him Fearless Fosdick after a cartoon detective drawn by Al Capp. The Nixon campaign was easily able to brush off these sallies from "the fastest, loosest tongue in the West." Nixon also avoided talking about Vietnam, implying that he had a "secret plan" to end the war, but would not reveal it for fear of hindering the president's peace efforts.

Nixon did encounter a challenge from the right, in the person of Alabama governor George Wallace. Running on an anti-integration, law-and-order platform, Wallace drew raucous crowds that thrilled to his earthy, aggressive style. Most of his support came from potential Nixon voters, although he also attracted Democrats. Nixon was nonetheless able to maintain a comfortable lead throughout the campaign.

Humphrey never completely recovered from the disasters of the convention. Although he later voiced his support of Daley's ferocious methods, he couldn't overcome voters' perception that mayhem followed the Democrats. At the same time he infuriated McCarthy, who refused to campaign for him. He also angered other potential supporters, who attended his rallies holding signs that said, "Mayor Daley for heart donor." As Democrats, the demonstrators concentrated their frustration on Humphrey. They largely ignored Nixon, who gave his speeches before sedate, respectful gatherings.

Humphrey finally picked up support when he began to distance himself from Johnson. In late September he told a Salt Lake City audience that he would unconditionally stop bombing North Vietnam if he thought it would shorten the war. Antiwar Democrats hailed his new attitude. At one Detroit appearance, a sign proclaimed, "HECKLERS FOR HUMPHREY—WE CAME BACK." Even McCarthy decided to endorse him. When Johnson halted the bombing in October in response to advances in the ongoing Paris peace negotiations, Humphrey got a further boost.

It was too late. Americans had already decided that they wanted a complete change. They elected Nixon by a comfortable margin. Democrats would take years to live down the calamitous happenings of the 1968 convention.

Pointy-Headed Bureaucrats

Unlike Humphrey, American Independent candidate George Wallace seemed to enjoy trading full-throated insults with hecklers. His favorite target was the "over-educated, ivory-tower folks with pointed heads" who looked down their noses at average Americans like Wallace and his supporters. An issue of *Science* that appeared shortly before the election noted, "Hardly a day goes by that Wallace fails to speak of 'pointy-headed professors who can't park their bicycles straight.'" This tactic evidently worked. Wallace captured 13 percent of the vote, winning five southern states.

Pointy heads was already a slang term for people with below-normal intelligence, presumably because their heads were too narrow to accommodate a full-size brain. Wallace applied the label to intellectual types who he believed were lacking in common sense, especially the bureaucrats running Washington. By the end of the 1968 campaign *pointy-headed bureaucrats* had become a common term.

Pointy heads has remained a popular insult, especially on the political right. Ironically, it has lost its "subnormal" connotation and now simply refers to any highly educated or scholarly person.

Peaceniks

The Yiddish word *nudnik*, meaning "a bore," had been familiar to Americans since the 1920s, but the Russian suffix *–nik* gained popularity when the Soviet Union launched the *Sputnik* satellite into outer space in 1957. A flurry of newly invented *–nik* words followed, most of them negative—*no-goodnik*, *neatnik*, and most famously, *beatnik*.

In the early 1960s, anti–Vietnam War agitators were labeled *peaceniks* by those who disapproved of their activities. It's one of the few *–nik* words still in use, usually as a pejorative.

Although Nixon beat Humphrey handily, and would win another term with equal ease, his political troubles were far from over. The traumas of Nixon's final years in office would give a name to the early 1970s—the Watergate era.

Beltway Bandits

WATERGATE AND AFTER

1972–1988

The early 1970s looked a lot like the late 1960s. Americans were still in Southeast Asia, although President Nixon's policy of "Vietnamization"—replacing U.S. troops with South Vietnamese—was beginning to take effect. Peaceniks were still demonstrating, and the Democratic Party was still in disarray. However, the political terrain was about to experience a seismic shift.

The first rumblings occurred during the summer before the 1972 presidential election. On June 17, five men were caught breaking into the Democratic Party's national headquarters, located in the exclusive Watergate apartment and office complex. The Watergate burglars took negative campaigning from the level of insulting words to illegal deeds, although the full scope of their "dirty tricks" campaign was not revealed until after the election.

When the situation did become clear, the fallout was severe. President Nixon resigned under threat of impeachment and several members of his administration stood trial for crimes related to the break-in. The Watergate scandal also had a long-term effect on voters. Many Americans were left disillusioned with politics and mistrustful of their elected officials. A popular post–Watergate era bumper sticker displayed the slogan "Nobody for president."

1972

RICHARD NIXON (REPUBLICAN) vs. GEORGE McGOVERN (DEMOCRAT)

Acid, Abortion, Amnesty

As the 1972 election season opened, President Nixon's reelection chances were uncertain. In spite of the "secret plan" touted during the previous election, he had not yet extricated the United States from the increasingly unpopular war in Vietnam. Americans— the mainstream as well as radicals—were becoming impatient. Fortunately for him, the Democrats continued to have image problems.

The 1972 Democratic nominating convention, held in Miami Beach in July, was not a replay of 1968. In its own way, however, it made just as negative an impression on American voters. Changes in how delegates were selected, especially a rule requiring that they reflect the demographic makeup of their state, drastically altered the look and feel of the event. Gone were the insiders—nearly all white men—who controlled the party machinery from smoke-filled back rooms. In their place were ethnic minorities, women, and young people. Or, as culturally conservative viewers at home saw it, Black Panthers, women's libbers, and radical hippies.

Many delegates were political neophytes, attending the convention as loyal supporters of South Dakota senator George McGovern, the presumptive nominee. Given a chance at the podium, they spoke about such normally forbidden topics as women's reproductive rights and gay rights.

The Democratic platform included a number of controversial proposals: immediate withdrawal of all Americans from Vietnam as soon as prisoners of war were released, amnesty for draft evaders, a guaranteed income program for the unemployed, school busing for desegregation, abolition of the death penalty, and—most scandalous to some—the right of all Americans "to make their own choice of life-styles and private habits." One observer noted that there would be no riots at the 1972 convention because "the people who rioted in Chicago are on the Platform Committee."

The Nixon campaign caricatured the Democratic platform as one of "Acid, Abortion, Amnesty." Neither LSD nor abortion was actually mentioned, nor did many of the more extreme proposals make it into the final platform. In fact, some of the Democrats' ideas were not that different from President Nixon's policies—for example, Nixon had proposed a guaranteed income program, although it failed to pass the Senate. His administration also expanded affirmative action laws.

These subtleties were lost on traditional Democratic voters. The televised convention convinced them that the Democratic Party was suddenly an unfamiliar place. "I think we lost the election at Miami," mourned one participant. The Republicans were easily able to portray McGovern as an extremist candidate, much as the Democrats had done to Goldwater in 1964.

In contrast Nixon, as a sitting president, was able to present himself as a competent and dignified leader. His groundbreaking visits to the Soviet Union and the People's Republic of China were much admired. He also boosted his popularity by announcing that he would end the draft.

The final blow to the McGovern campaign was the revelation that the vice presidential candidate, Missouri senator Tom Eagleton, had been treated three times for mental health problems, and had undergone electroshock therapy. Shortly after the story broke, McGovern announced that he was "1,000 percent for Tom Eagleton" and had no intention of dropping him from the ticket.

Others were not so sure. Major newspapers, even those that supported McGovern, began to call for Eagleton to be replaced. Many Democratic Party leaders felt the same. Eventually, under pressure from the party and his own staff, McGovern asked Eagleton to step down. He then offered the position to several people unsuccessfully before Kennedy in-law Sargent Shriver finally agreed to take Eagleton's place on the ticket. The Republicans capitalized on these events by attacking McGovern as indecisive and lacking in political courage.

McGovern was unable to rebound from this final disaster. His loss to Nixon was even more lopsided than Goldwater's loss to Johnson in 1964. He lost every state except Massachusetts, even his home state of South Dakota. When the Watergate scandal broke shortly after the beginning of President Nixon's second term, bumper stickers began appearing that said, "Don't blame me—I'm from Massachusetts." On Election Day, however, the situation held little humor for the Democrats.

The Imperial Presidency

Features of an imperial presidency include reliance on a tight coterie of advisers, secrecy in decision making, and disregard for the Constitution, especially the provision that Congress rather than the president holds the power to declare war. To Nixon's opponents, *imperial presidency* seemed like an apt description of his governing style. The phrase began appearing in connection with the president around 1971. *New York Times* columnist Tom Wicker wrote in a January 5, 1972, column: "Publication [of government documents] is one of the few remaining checks on the foreign policy powers of the imperial presidency."

The term gained wide currency with the 1973 appearance of Arthur M. Schlesinger's book *The Imperial Presidency.* The book is not specifically about President Nixon, although he figures in it. It traces the growth of presidential power over time. Administrations both before and after Nixon have been labeled imperial presidencies, including those of Lyndon Johnson and George W. Bush.

Dirty Tricks Campaign

Like *imperial presidency*, the term *dirty tricks campaign* is often associated with the Nixon administration, although the phrase *dirty tricks*, meaning "underhanded or deceitful tactics," has been around since the nineteenth century. In fact, dirty tricks in one form or another have been a feature of American elections since Thomas Jefferson and John Adams battled to replace George Washington in 1796.

The Committee to Re-Elect the President (familiarly known as CREEP from its initials) arguably took dirty tricks campaigning to new depths. The committee started operations well before the 1972 general election. During the Democratic primaries the early frontrunner, Senator Edmund Muskie of Maine, was laid low by a series of smears that were later found to be orchestrated by Republican hatchet man Donald Segretti.

The most famous attack was a spurious letter to the *Manchester (NH) Union Leader* claiming that Muskie had referred to French Canadians in that state with the insulting term Canucks. While defending himself from this charge during an outdoor news conference, Muskie made matters worse by appearing to shed tears. He later claimed that he had merely choked with anger. The falling snow might also have contributed to his wet-cheeked appearance. Whatever the extenuating circumstances, voters were left with the impression that Muskie couldn't take the pressure of a presidential campaign. He made a disappointing showing in the New Hampshire primary.

Shortly afterward, Florida primary voters received letters on fake Muskie campaign stationery. These falsely accused other Democratic candidates of offenses ranging from drunk driving to sex with minors. Billboards also appeared on Florida highways with incendiary captions such as, "Help Muskie in Busing More Children Now." Muskie steadily lost ground. Eventually he quit the race, opening the way for George McGovern, considered less of a threat to Nixon.

The Committee to Re-Elect the President was also responsible for the bungled break-in at the Democrats' national campaign headquarters. At first, the arrest of the Watergate burglars caused few ripples. Only after the election—when one of the men involved implicated the committee during his trial—did Americans begin to realize that the president or members of his staff may have been directly involved in illegal campaign activities. Senator Howard Baker asked the crucial question: "What did the president know and when did he know it?"

Disaster loomed when a presidential aide revealed that Nixon routinely taped his Oval Office conversations. The Senate committee investigating the Watergate incident subpoenaed the tapes, which made it clear that the president had known about the break-in and subsequent cover-up from an early point. The Senate hearings also brought to light a broader pattern of dirty tricks, such as the illegal wiretapping of opponents. With impeachment almost certain, Nixon resigned the presidency on August 9, 1974.

Dirty tricks campaign is now a permanent part of the political vocabulary, especially during election season. It is generally interpreted as an attack that goes above and beyond the usual negative advertising.

Nattering Nabobs of Negativism

Nixon's vice president, Spiro Agnew, liked to liven up his speeches with alliterative insults. While working with Agnew on a 1970 speech for the California state Republican convention, Nixon speechwriter William Safire coined the memorable phrase *nattering nabobs of negativism*. According to Safire, he offered the vice president a choice of alliterative phrases. Agnew chose to use them both, but only the *nabobs* phrase really caught on.

The subject of Agnew's attack was the press corps. He told his audience, "In the United States today we have more than our share of the nattering nabobs of negativism. They have formed

---

Nattering nabobs of negativism has been detached from its original context and can now be used to describe people with a negative attitude on any subject. One example from the sports world is this line from a January 20, 2010, column on *NBC Sports* online: "[Michigan football coach Rich Rodriguez] is, the nattering nabobs of negativism insist, rebuilding an elite program with second-tier players."

---

their own 4-H Club—the hopeless, hysterical hypochondriacs of history." In Agnew's opinion, the press was damaging the Nixon administration with deliberately negative reporting and editorial doomsaying, especially about the Vietnam War.

1976

JIMMY CARTER (DEMOCRAT) VS. GERALD FORD (REPUBLICAN)

When President Nixon resigned in August 1974, Vice President Gerald Ford stepped into the position for the remainder of Nixon's term. (Former vice president Spiro Agnew left office in October 1973 after being charged with accepting bribes while governor of Maryland.) Soon after becoming president, Ford granted Nixon a blanket pardon, angering many voters. They saw the 1976 election as a chance to reject the Watergate era's "insider" politics.

Jimmy Carter, the former governor of Georgia, was the quintessential "outsider" candidate. He was virtually unknown outside his state. During his strenuous cross-country primary campaign, he often began speeches with the line, "My name is Jimmy Carter and I'm running for president." Many Americans considered his lack of prior experience a plus, especially when the Republicans endorsed the status quo by choosing President Ford as their candidate.

Although Carter started the campaign with a big lead, he made some missteps—among them, an ill-advised interview with *Playboy* magazine—that allowed Ford to pull nearly even in the polls by

Election Day. However, Ford also committed campaign blunders, such as his insistence during one debate that the Soviet Union did not dominate Eastern Europe. In the end, Americans' eagerness to put Watergate behind them allowed Carter to eke out a narrow win.

Beltway Bandits

The Beltway is a loop highway encircling Washington, DC, built during the 1950s to divert traffic around the city. By the 1970s, *inside the Beltway* meant the tightly enclosed world of insider politics in the nation's capital. Among the insiders were private contractors—"bandits" who charged the government exorbitant fees for their work. One of the first examples of *Beltway bandits* comes from a June 1978 *Harper's* article exploring the sources of Washingtonians' income: "There are also the consultants—the 'beltway bandits,' as they are sometimes called. These are the people who do government work for a fee."

The disparaging term caught on, maybe because Americans were more aware—and disapproving—of government backroom deals after Watergate. It is still current. A *Fortune* article for January 26, 2004, includes the line, "Halliburton has been called . . . a no-good Beltway Bandit."

Drinking the Kool-Aid

The tragedy of cult leader Jim Jones and his Jonestown followers gave rise to a political sneer that is still popular decades after the event. Jones was founder and head of the Peoples Temple. He and several hundred temple members moved to Guyana in 1977, where they established Jonestown. In November 1978, a U.S. congressional delegation, headed by Representative Leo Ryan of California, visited Jonestown to investigate reports of cultish practices. As the delegation was boarding planes to return home, several Jones loyalists drove onto the airstrip and opened fire, killing Representative Ryan and four others. Later that day, Jones and over nine hundred church members committed mass suicide by drinking cyanide-laced Flavor-aid.

Shortly after the Jonestown disaster, references to the mindless drinking of true believers' Kool-Aid began to appear in print. (Kool-Aid is much better known in the United States than Flavor-aid, which probably accounts for the switch in brands.) An early figurative use of the phrase appeared in a September 23, 1985, *Washington Post* article about Representative Dick Gephardt: "What he didn't want, [Press Secretary Don] Foley was telling Joyce Aboussie, Gephardt's campaign manager, was 'what I call the politics of Jim Jones, you know, that "let's drink the Kool-Aid" kind of downer.'"

Drinking the Kool-Aid means "committing yourself unquestioningly to a person, cause, or set of beliefs," no matter how problematic they may be in some respects. Political partisans frequently dismiss opponents' ideas as so much poisoned Kool-Aid.

In recent years, *drink the Kool-Aid* often appears with an adjective, as in this phrase from the October 6, 2002, *New York Times Magazine*: "People in this city were initially reluctant to drink the New Economy Kool-Aid."

1980

RONALD REAGAN (REPUBLICAN) VS. JIMMY CARTER (DEMOCRAT) VS. JOHN ANDERSON (INDEPENDENT)

ABC: Anybody but Carter

The 1980 presidential campaign was notable for a lack of enthusiasm for either candidate. Democratic incumbent Jimmy Carter was beset by problems. The country was struggling with "stagflation"— a stagnant economy plus inflation—high unemployment, and rising oil prices. The president was also facing an ongoing hostage crisis.

In November 1979, Iranian student revolutionaries stormed the American embassy in Tehran, taking over fifty Americans hostage. After failed negotiations and a disastrous rescue attempt, they remained in captivity as election season neared. At one point, Carter's approval ratings sank to 21 percent, lower than Nixon's during the Watergate investigation.

The president's reelection troubles started before the Democratic nominating convention. Although Carter won enough primaries to capture a majority of the delegates, polls showed that a significant number of Democrats considered him unelectable. An "ABC" movement began to build—Anybody but Carter.

One alternative was Senator Ted Kennedy, who was close behind Carter in numbers of delegates. Even after Carter gathered enough votes to clinch the nomination, Kennedy refused to concede. Instead, he fought for an open convention that would allow the delegates to vote as they pleased. A "Draft Muskie" campaign also took hold. Senator Edmund Muskie's supporters argued that Muskie was polling better than Carter against the probable Republican candidate, former California governor Ronald Reagan. Carter eventually overcame these challenges to win the nomination, but the lack of unity in the convention hall was palpable.

Reagan's progress toward the Republican nomination was much smoother. Although the field started out crowded—Republicans smelled incumbent blood in the water—Reagan collected enough delegates by the time of the convention to win the nomination on the first ballot. The party was united and confident. They believed they could easily defeat Carter. Their slogans, alluding to Carter's former life as a peanut farmer, verged on the lighthearted—"Shell that peanut," "Import peanuts, export Carter," and "Elephants eat peanuts."

Reagan himself also presented a relaxed and confident demeanor. Although his positions were often harsh—for instance, he called the Soviet Union "the Evil Empire" and railed against "welfare queens"—his personal style was friendly. He sometimes made self-deprecating jokes.

In contrast, when Carter attacked Reagan's positions he came off as shrill. He accused Reagan of wanting nuclear war and of fomenting racism. He warned that with Reagan as president, "Americans might be separated, black from white, Jew from Christian, North from South, rural from urban." News commentators began talking about "the meanness issue."

The nadir for Carter came during the candidates' debate. Reagan was calm and self-assured, while Carter appeared ill at ease and angry. Late in the debate, Carter attacked Reagan's opposition to social welfare programs, pointing out that Reagan had started his political career campaigning against Medicare. Reagan replied with a sad smile, "There you go again." This riposte became the most memorable line of the evening. It conveyed to the audience that Reagan was patiently enduring repeated unfair attacks.

As with the Nixon–Kennedy debates, Reagan's poise in front of the cameras gave him a real advantage. The debate persuaded many wary voters that Reagan's views were not as extreme as Carter claimed. Still, people were not so much in favor of Reagan as opposed to Carter. Third-party candidate John Anderson, when questioned on his role as a "spoiler," asked, "What's to spoil? Spoil the chances of two men at least half the country doesn't want?"

On Election Day, only slightly over half of eligible voters went to the polls. Anderson received a respectable 7 percent of the vote, but the country went overwhelmingly for Reagan. The miserable economy exerted more force than Carter's meanness attacks.

Voodoo Economics

The term *voodoo economics* illustrates the dangers of attacking fellow party members too pointedly during the primaries. George H. W. Bush invented this description of Reagan's economic policies when competing with him for the 1980 Republican nomination. After Reagan won the nomination and invited Bush to join him on the ticket, Bush's pithy coinage didn't go to waste. The Democrats mentioned it frequently during the general campaign.

Voodoo economics was Bush's way of describing what is usually called supply-side economics or, more negatively, trickle-down economics. Supply-siders such as Reagan believed that lower tax rates, especially for businesses and the rich, would stimulate investment. In turn, more investment would create jobs. The government's income from taxes would increase in spite of lower tax rates because more wealth would be created.

Skeptics considered supply-side theory a kind of magical thinking. On April 11, 1980, the *Philadelphia Inquirer* reported Bush's new term for it: "Bush warned a friendly crowd of students not to be deceived by Reagan's voodoo economics." Anderson also suggested that Reagan was promising to perform magic. During an early debate he asked the rhetorical question, "How do you balance the budget, cut taxes and increase defense spending at the same time? . . . You do it with mirrors."

Although *voodoo economics* started out as a specific reference to supply-side economics, it can now signify any economic policy that the speaker considers misguided. A November 14, 2007, *Long Beach (CA) Press-Telegram* article told readers: "Politicians habitually practice voodoo economics, making rhetorical, logic-free connections between what they do and the health of the economy."

October Surprises

Since 1980, any unexpected political development that occurs close to an election is labeled an *October surprise*, especially if one side gains an advantage from it. During the 1980 presidential campaign the term described Republican worries that President Carter might manipulate events so the American hostages in Tehran would be released just before the election. That achievement could have boosted the president's popularity enough to give him a second term. Reporting on this concern, the September 1, 1980, *New York Times* said, "Republicans worry about an 'October surprise' in foreign policy."

As it turned out, the hostage situation continued to be a problem for Carter. The hostages were not freed until inauguration day, minutes after Reagan took office. This timing led some to believe that the Reagan campaign, rather than the Carter administration, had been the ones manipulating events. Several books and articles have argued that Reagan's people struck a secret deal with Iran to hold the hostages until after the election. The Senate Committee on Foreign Relations concluded in 1992 that these claims were unfounded.

Negative October surprises in the past couple of decades have ranged from calamities in foreign affairs to embarrassing revelations about the candidates' private lives.

The Teflon-Coated Presidency

Teflon is a DuPont trademark for a nonstick coating for cookware. Some political observers thought that President Ronald Reagan displayed a similar nonstick quality because his administration's scandals and missteps seemed to roll harmlessly off his back. For example, early in Reagan's first term, the economy suffered the worst recession since the 1930s. Yet the president's personal popularity remained as high as ever.

Colorado representative Patricia Schroeder invented the non-stick characterization of the president. During the August 2, 1983, House session, she commented: "Mr. Speaker, after carefully watching Ronald Reagan, he is attempting a great breakthrough in political technology—he has been perfecting the Teflon-coated Presidency. He sees to it that nothing sticks to him." Although negatives may not have stuck to him, the label did. References to Reagan's Teflon coating began to appear in newspapers, such as this commentary from the *Atlanta Journal-Constitution* for May 20, 1984: "Reagan is said to live a charmed political life as the proprietor of a Teflon-coated presidency."

The label then began to be applied to other politicians who were skilled at avoiding blame. A *New Yorker* article from the January 28, 1985, issue says of New York mayor Ed Koch: "Like President Reagan, the Mayor is celebrated for . . . distancing himself as far as possible from whatever may have gone wrong. . . . The executive director of the largest local public-employees' union has called him 'the Teflon mayor.'"

The term *Teflon-coated* still resonates in politics. *New York Times* columnist Frank Rich used it on July 11, 2009, to describe former vice presidential candidate Sarah Palin: "She has the Teflon-coated stature among Republicans that [former Massachusetts governor Mitt] Romney can only fantasize about."

The Sleaze Factor

The sleaze factor first appeared as a chapter title in the 1983 book *Gambling with History: Ronald Reagan in the White House,* by Laurence I. Barrett. Barrett was writing about various Reagan associates whose backgrounds included questionable business dealings. Democrats adopted *sleaze factor* to label what they saw as a pattern of low-level corruption in the administration. Former vice president Walter Mondale, while campaigning for the Democratic nomination in 1984, attacked the Reagan administration as having a "sleaze factor" and "a tawdry record of unethical conduct."

The sleaze factor now refers generally to the scandalous or sordid aspect of a situation. It doesn't apply exclusively to politics. A June 9, 2008, Associated Press article on Kansas casinos includes the line, "There is a sleaze factor associated with the gambling industry."

Chicken Hawks

In the 1960s, supporters of the Vietnam War were commonly referred to as hawks. The term might or might not be negative, depending on the speaker's point of view. In the 1980s, a new breed of bird appeared—the chicken hawk. This term applied to politicians, typically male, who had not served in Vietnam, but who nonetheless favored American military interventions overseas. Unlike *hawk, chicken hawk* is always an insult. It implies that in spite of hawkish attitudes, a person is too chicken to fight.

An early use of the word appeared in a June 16, 1986, *New Republic* article about evolving attitudes toward the Vietnam War:

"so-called 'war wimps' or 'chicken hawks'—prominent Americans helping to spread war fever today who avoided service during Vietnam." At first the term specifically referred to men who had avoided the Vietnam draft. More recently it has broadened to mean someone who tends to support going to war, but has never served in the military.

1984

RONALD REAGAN (REPUBLICAN) VS. WALTER MONDALE (DEMOCRAT)

The 1984 election was boring, even for the participants themselves. Democratic candidate Walter Mondale complained to an aide, "This campaign is *glacial*." President Reagan's reelection was almost a foregone conclusion. He remained broadly popular, although some wondered whether, at seventy-three, he was getting too old for the job. His occasional public confusion and memory lapses reinforced this concern. However, he was able to brush the issue aside with good-humored joking, just as he had brushed aside Jimmy Carter's attacks four years earlier.

Mondale lacked Reagan's personal charm. His campaign speeches—mainly against the ballooning budget deficit—failed to ignite the voters. His call for a tax hike to offset the deficit allowed Reagan to attack him as a typical high-taxing, high-spending Democrat. Mondale's choice of New York congresswoman Geraldine Ferraro as a running mate—the first female vice presidential candidate—gave his campaign a temporary boost, but questions about Ferraro's husband's finances soon negated that advantage.

Reagan's reelection victory was one of the most lopsided ever. He won 525 electoral votes to Mondale's 13.

1988

George H. W. Bush (Republican) vs. Michael Dukakis (Democrat)

The Dukakis/Willie Horton Team

The 1988 presidential race is most remembered for hitting what some considered an all-time low in negative campaigning. The contest between Republican vice president George H. W. Bush and Democratic former Massachusetts governor Michael Dukakis was short on discussion of substantive issues and long on personal attacks, unsupported rumors, charges, and countercharges.

The most notorious attack came from the Republicans—a series of television spots known as "the Willie Horton Ads." Willie Horton (known as William until the creation of the ads) was a convicted murderer serving a life sentence in a Massachusetts penitentiary. During Dukakis's term as governor, Horton was released as part of a weekend furlough program. While free, he raped a woman and brutally attacked her fiancé. He was later recaptured and imprisoned in Maryland.

The Bush campaign used the Horton case to accuse Dukakis

of being soft on crime. Bush began mentioning Horton during speeches—for example, saying that the former governor let "murderers out on vacation to terrorize innocent people." He said that while actor Clint Eastwood's Dirty Harry character told criminals, "Go ahead, make my day," Dukakis told them, "Go ahead, have a nice weekend."

The Republicans flooded the airwaves with Willie Horton commercials. A mug shot of Horton appeared on-screen while an announcer intoned, "Weekend passes. Dukakis on crime." The ad's creator, Larry McCarthy, commented that Horton's picture—that of a heavily bearded, scowling black man—represented "every suburban mother's greatest fear." Another frequently played spot showed a line of prisoners walking through a turnstile, into prison and then back out again.

Accusing opponents of committing shameful follies while in office was hardly new—such charges have been routine since Washington was president. Nor was playing on voter prejudices a novelty. The Democrats beat John Frémont in 1856 and the Republicans beat Al Smith in 1928 using similar tactics. However, modern technology allowed Republicans to bombard voters with a more intensive and widespread mudslinging campaign than in previous eras.

State Republican committees followed the national committee's lead. Illinois Republicans distributed a flyer with the line: "All the murderers and rapists and drug pushers and child molesters in Massachusetts vote for Michael Dukakis." Texas voters received a "Get out of jail free" card in the mail that read: "Michael Dukakis is the killer's best friend and the decent honest citizen's worst enemy." Maryland Republicans sent out a fund-raising letter warning against the Dukakis/Willie Horton team: "Is This Your Pro-Family Team for 1988?" Soon after the election, *Willie Hortonize* began appearing in print as a synonym for an all-out smear campaign.

These attacks were more effective because Dukakis did not at first respond to them. After some delay, campaign manager Susan Estrich started pointing out that the furlough program, operating in over forty states, had been initiated in Massachusetts by a Republican governor. She also noted that when Ronald Reagan was governor of California, a criminal on a seventy-two-hour furlough murdered a Los Angeles police officer.

Bush himself had founded halfway houses for Houston convicts when he was a Texas congressman during the late 1960s. In 1982 one halfway house inmate raped and murdered a minister's wife. The Democrats eventually turned these facts into a commercial of their own, but their belated response did not have nearly the impact of the original ads.

The Bush campaign also charged Dukakis with being an elitist Harvard-educated liberal and unpatriotic to boot. They based this attack on the fact that Dukakis vetoed a bill that would have required Massachusetts public school students to recite the Pledge of Allegiance. Dukakis pointed out in vain that the law would have been unconstitutional. Again, the explanation didn't receive nearly as much publicity as the original accusation. Nor were Democratic reminders that Bush had attended Yale, also an Ivy League school, of much avail.

Bush was among the first politicians to turn *liberal*—traditionally a descriptive label for a particular approach to government—into an insult (for more, see Chapter 8).

The Dukakis campaign also indulged in smear tactics, although on a lesser scale. Staff members spread the rumor that Bush had had an affair with his former secretary. Democrats also attempted to connect Bush with various Reagan administration scandals. Coming late in the campaign, none of these attacks had a chance to gain much traction.

Eligible voters continued to be apathetic. An even lower percentage turned out for the 1988 election than had voted in 1980. However, a solid majority of those who felt moved to vote preferred Bush. The result may have been the same without "the Willie Horton Ads." Bush held the advantage of having been vice president to the popular Reagan, and many voters also viewed him as more personable than Dukakis. However, the ads were undoubtedly an effective reinforcement of Republican campaign themes.

You're No Jack Kennedy

Republican vice presidential candidate Dan Quayle faced concerns about his age and relative lack of experience. The Indiana senator was forty-one, but looked younger. At sixty-seven, Democratic vice presidential candidate Lloyd Bentsen was old enough to be Quayle's father. During a debate between the two men shortly before the election, Quayle answered a question about his age by pointing out that he had nearly as much senatorial experience as John Kennedy had when Kennedy ran for president.

Bentsen flattened his opponent with this response: "Senator, I served with Jack Kennedy, I knew Jack Kennedy, Jack Kennedy was a friend of mine. Senator, you're no Jack Kennedy."

Amid audience shouts and applause, an obviously discomfited Quayle murmured, "That was really uncalled for, Senator."

Bentsen replied, "You are the one that was making the comparison, Senator."

Something about Bentsen's withering putdown appealed to Americans. Democrats turned the moment into a television ad. Soon the phrase was circulating as the punch line of jokes. The retort, "You're no [any name here]" was a sure laugh getter.

The comment *You're no Jack Kennedy* remained potent long after other aspects of the 1988 campaign were forgotten. Four years later, during the Republican convention, former president Reagan drew on the line to joke about his age while attacking Democratic nominee Bill Clinton. Reagan told a laughing audience, "This fellow they've nominated claims he's the new Thomas Jefferson. Well, let me tell you something. I knew Thomas Jefferson. He was a friend of mine. And Governor, you're no Thomas Jefferson."

Bill Clinton may not have been Thomas Jefferson, but he was about to make Reagan's former running mate, George H. W. Bush, a one-term president. Clinton's election ushered in a turbulent era of attack politics.

★ 8 ★

Latte Liberals and Wingnuts

B y the 1990s mudslinging had gone ballistic. The proliferation of talking heads on radio and television, not to mention the Internet's capability for instant scandal mongering, ensured that the smallest misspoken word or most trivial piece of negative gossip would get instant nationwide play.

Besides the now-standard televised debates, candidates in the 1990s began visiting talk shows as well as participating in call-in programs and electronic town hall meetings, where they interacted directly with voters. All this public exposure offered unprecedented opportunities for politicians both to attack opponents and reveal their own weak spots.

Modern electronics certainly played a part in creating a firestorm of negativity against President Bill Clinton. In 1998 Clinton became the second president after Andrew Johnson to be impeached. Like Johnson, he was acquitted. However, the Clinton impeachment was a much more public affair, triggering nonstop media coverage, leaked revelations of lurid facts, and thousands of Internet postings.

1992

BILL CLINTON (DEMOCRAT) VS. GEORGE H. W. BUSH (REPUBLICAN) VS. ROSS PEROT (INDEPENDENT)

It's the Economy, Stupid

In 1990, most political observers would have said that President Bush was a shoo-in for reelection. After successfully leading an international effort to drive Iraqi invaders out of Kuwait, his approval rating rose to 89 percent. Unfortunately, in the two years between the end of the Gulf War and the beginning of the 1992 election cycle, the American economy fell into a recession. Tens of thousands of jobs disappeared. At the same time, the national deficit skyrocketed. To top it off, Bush broke his 1988 campaign promise of "Read my lips: no new taxes," infuriating Republican supporters.

The Democratic challenger, Arkansas governor Bill Clinton, quickly zeroed in on what he saw as the contest's most powerful issue. A sign posted on the wall of his campaign headquarters in

Little Rock was a reminder: "The economy, stupid." This slogan was modeled on a popular office poster of the time: "Keep it simple, stupid." Clinton supporters adopted "It's the economy, stupid!" as their rallying cry.

Clinton scored points during debates and town hall meetings by speaking feelingly about the economic hardships of ordinary people. When challenged to name the prices of several grocery staples, he was able to answer correctly. In contrast, Bush often fumbled this type of question. He further damaged himself during one debate when television cameras caught him glancing at his watch while Clinton spoke with an audience member about lost jobs. It was a "there you go again" moment. Democrats hammered on the theme that Bush "didn't get" real people's economic problems.

The president also came under pressure from third-party candidate Ross Perot, running mainly on an antideficit platform. Perot, who was known for his trenchant way with words, ridiculed Bush's economic policies as "deep voodoo." This alluded to Bush's coinage, *voodoo economics*—now come back to haunt him—combined with a reference to the much-derided Bush usage *deep doo-doo*, meaning "serious trouble." Perot also opposed the projected free-trade agreement with Mexico. He warned Americans that they would hear the "giant sucking sound" of their jobs being dragged over the border.

The Bush campaign targeted Clinton as a "philandering, pot-smoking draft dodger," forcing him to spend campaigning time explaining his past history. He admitted that he had tried marijuana while at Oxford, but insisted—to the incredulity of some contemporaries—that he "didn't inhale." He denied dodging the draft, saying that he drew a high lottery number and was never called. He even provided an affidavit from his draft board confirming that he had not received special treatment. This information did not deter one Republican speechmaker from referring to him as "Chicken Little of Little Rock."

A thornier challenge was dealing with what a member of his campaign staff coarsely described as "bimbo eruptions"—recurring rumors that Clinton was a womanizer. The *Star* tabloid printed a story claiming that Clinton committed adultery with several women while governor of Arkansas. When he and his wife, Hillary, addressed the issue during an interview on the television program *60 Minutes*, viewers were favorably impressed with the Clintons' frank discussion of their marriage. A majority declared to follow-up pollsters that the press had no business prying into the candidate's personal life.

In spite of the flurry of bad publicity, Clinton's positive ratings remained steady. Frustrated Bush supporters began referring to him as Slick Willie. His Teflon quality was probably enhanced by the country's ongoing economic problems. Voters who were disturbed by Willie Horton commercials in 1988 were not as susceptible to negative political ads in 1992—they had more immediate worries.

Toward the end of the campaign, both sides began hurling accusations of inaccuracy and downright lying. The Bush campaign issued press releases titled "Distortion of the Day." Bush repeatedly attacked Clinton on "the trust issue" during speeches. Clinton countered, "Every time Bush talks about trust it makes chills run up and down my spine." He declared that the Bush campaign had been the most reckless with the truth of any in modern American history.

To add to Bush's troubles Ross Perot, who had dropped out of the contest in July, suddenly reentered the fray in October with stories that he had stopped campaigning because the "Republican dirty tricks group" had threatened to smear his daughter and ruin her wedding day. Bush denied the charge, but it added to the negative fallout.

As Election Day neared and the president continued to trail in the polls, he spoke hopefully of being the Comeback Kid. He reminded his supporters of Harry Truman's astonishing upset victory over Thomas Dewey in 1948, prompting Truman's daughter Margaret to issue a statement in the August 27 *Washington Post*: "I would say to George Bush, 'You are no Harry Truman.'"

Sadly for Bush, that analysis proved true. With the highest turnout of eligible voters since 1972, Clinton received nearly 43 percent of the vote to Bush's 37 percent. Perot garnered nearly 19 percent, the most votes for any third-party candidate since Theodore Roosevelt in 1912. Like other candidates before him, Clinton benefited from a divided opposition.

The Bubba Vote

A much-discussed constituency during the 1992 election was that of conservative white male southerners, often lumped together under the dismissive heading, "the Bubba vote." The word *bubba*, a diminutive of *brother*, is innocuous in itself. Southerners use it both as a term of affection and a nickname. However, in its political context the term implied a negative stereotype—the reactionary, racist southern man.

Politicians may have viewed bubbas in a less-than-flattering light, but they still wanted to capture the votes of this influential demographic. When southerner Pat Buchanan challenged President Bush for the Republican nomination, the *Wall Street Journal* noted that Buchanan was "making inroads into the 'Bubba' vote—conservative whites, many of them Democrats."

Both Bill Clinton and his running mate, Al Gore, were from the South (Arkansas and Tennessee, respectively). While campaigning, Clinton embraced the positive aspects of being a bubba, saying during one interview: "There's a little bubba in both of us—in the sense that we both came from small towns, where people have old-fashioned values and want their country to be the best country in the world—and I don't think that's all bad." They were humorously known in some quarters as "the Double Bubba ticket."

Astroturf Movements

Astroturf movements are to grassroots movements what Astro-Turf—an artificial surface first used in the Houston Astrodome—is to grass. *Grassroots* has been a term for a rank-and-file political movement since the beginning of the twentieth century. Astroturf movements did not come along until much later.

The name describes expressions of voter opinion that critics suspect are being deliberately orchestrated. One of the earliest

> **Besides the bubba vote, other voting blocs discussed during the 1990s were soccer moms—suburban women who spent their time driving their children to soccer games and other after-school activities—and waitress moms—blue-collar working women. The 2004 election saw the NASCAR dad—a relative of the bubbas who enjoyed stock car racing—and the security mom—a woman whose main concern was protecting her children from terrorists. Although none of these labels is necessarily an insult, they all carry the suggestion of stereotypes whose voting patterns can be predicted from their lifestyles.**

uses appeared in the *Washington Post* for August 7, 1985: "'A fellow from Texas can tell the difference between grass roots and Astro Turf,' Sen. Lloyd Bentsen (D-Tex.) said of his mountain of cards and letters. . . . 'This is generated mail.'"

Astroturf movements proliferated in the late 1990s when email, computer-generated telephone calls, and other technological advances made churning out thousands of form messages a fairly straightforward matter. People who wouldn't bother to write an original letter are often willing to fill in their name and address and click "Send." This quotation from a 2002 *New York Times* article demonstrates that *Astroturf* can be a verb as well as a noun: "'I don't think they're Astroturfing us,' said John Feehery, a spokesman for House Speaker J. Dennis Hastert."

1996

BILL CLINTON (DEMOCRAT) VS. ROBERT DOLE (REPUBLICAN)

Bill Clinton easily gained a second term. The economy was healthy, and the president remained in favor with most of the electorate. Clinton's adoption of certain traditionally Republican issues, such as welfare reform and a balanced federal budget, made it difficult for his opponent, Kansas senator Bob Dole, to campaign effectively against him. The seventy-two-year-old Dole also seemed a bit behind the times to many younger voters.

Ross Perot made another run for the presidency, this time on the Reform Party ticket. His campaign had much less impact the second time around. Dole would have lost the popular vote even if every Perot supporter had voted for Dole instead. As it was, Clinton won comfortably, with 379 electoral votes to Dole's 159.

Vast Right-Wing Conspiracy

While in office, President Clinton endured an extensive and free-ranging exploration into his business and personal life. Early in his presidency, Attorney General Janet Reno appointed independent counsel Kenneth Starr to investigate the Clintons' involvement in a real estate project called Whitewater.

When the Whitewater investigation failed to turn up evidence of wrongdoing, Starr began branching into other areas. These included the suicide of White House counsel Vincent Foster, the firing of White House Travel Office staff (known as Travelgate), and allegations by former Arkansas state employee Paula Jones that then-Governor Clinton had sexually harassed her. While pursuing the Jones case, Starr acquired evidence that President Clinton had been intimately involved with White House intern Monica Lewinsky. During his deposition for the Jones lawsuit, Clinton gave evasive answers when questioned about Lewinsky. This incident eventually led to his impeachment on perjury charges.

First Lady Hillary Clinton, appearing on the *Today Show* after the Lewinsky scandal broke, voiced her belief that ongoing efforts to discredit the president were the work of an organized group: "Look at the very people who are involved in this—they have popped up in other settings. . . . This vast right-wing conspiracy that has been conspiring against my husband since the day he announced for president."

Conservatives noted the phrase. When it became clear that the president had indeed had a relationship with Lewinsky, they used it to mock the Clintons. One pundit wrote a bestselling book titled *The Vast Right-Wing Conspiracy Handbook*. Merchandise stamped "VRWC" went on sale.

The pendulum swung back to some extent in later years. Several writers have published evidence of a concerted right-wing effort to bring down the president, although the individuals involved may not have conspired together beforehand.

2000

GEORGE W. BUSH (REPUBLICAN) VS. AL GORE (DEMOCRAT)

Sore Loserman

The 2000 presidential election brought echoes of 1876—an extremely close contest that tested the limits of the electoral system. As with Hayes and Tilden (see Chapter 3), neither candidate in 2000 emerged from the voting process with a clear majority of electoral votes. And once again, Florida was at the center of the controversy.

The campaign itself was uneventful—neither man generated high excitement among the voters. Democratic candidate Al Gore had the advantage of being vice president during a time of prosperity, but the scandals of the Clinton White House led him to distance himself from the administration. His stiff, wonkish persona was also a campaigning hindrance. Republican candidate George W. Bush—running for the office eight years after his father left it—presented a folksier image. However, his slips of the tongue and occasionally weak grasp of issues provided fodder for the Democrats. The race was tight.

The real action started after most of the votes were in. By Election Day evening, Gore had clearly won the popular vote, but he was still three electoral votes short of a majority—267 to Bush's 246. Still unassigned were Florida's 25 electoral votes, enough to put either candidate over the top. Television news programs added to the suspense with dueling predictions. First they called the state for Gore, then for Bush, and finally admitted that the vote was too close to call. Gore telephoned Bush early in the evening to concede, then awkwardly called him again later to "unconcede."

The closeness of the vote automatically triggered a machine recount, which gave Bush a lead of around three hundred votes. Meanwhile, stories of voting irregularities kept surfacing. Problems included a hard-to-understand "butterfly" ballot, voting machines that subtracted votes instead of adding them, punch-card ballots that failed to register a clear vote, and complaints from hundreds of African American Floridians (who tend to vote Democratic) that they had been erroneously dropped from the voter rolls. The Gore team decided to ask for a hand recount in three counties.

Florida secretary of state Katherine Harris, who was also acting as cochair of Bush's state campaign, refused to extend the November 14 deadline for reporting nonmilitary vote counts. The Democrats then went to the Florida Supreme Court, which overruled Harris. The recounts began amid chaos and mutual accusations of vote tampering.

The most bizarre incident occurred when a crowd of Republican staffers—later called the Brooks Brothers protesters—charged into Dade County's tabulation room crying, "Stop the count!" They created enough turmoil to force the recount to a halt. Outside the building, groups of Bush and Gore supporters brandished competing signs: "Sore Loserman 2000" (a play on the Democratic ticket, Gore–Lieberman) versus "George W. Bush Is a Moron." People from both camps worried that after two weeks with no final result, the American people were running out of patience.

(The 1876 Hayes–Tilden election wasn't resolved until March 1877, but nineteenth-century citizens were used to waiting weeks, or even months, for news of election results.)

When the new deadline of November 26 arrived with the recounts still uncompleted, Harris certified Bush the winner. The Democrats challenged Harris's decision, asking the Florida Supreme Court to allow the counting to continue. They also asked for hand counts of uncounted ballots in all sixty-seven Florida counties. When the state court approved these requests, the Republicans appealed to the U.S. Supreme Court to stop the proceedings on the grounds that they violated Bush's constitutional right to equal protection of the laws.

Normally, voting matters are left to the state's jurisdiction. This time, in an unprecedented move, the Supreme Court agreed to hear the case. On December 12 the justices voted 5–4 along partisan lines to end the recounts, effectively awarding Bush the presidency. The election was over after thirty-six days.

As in 1876, some on the losing side remained unreconciled. The inauguration drew protesters wielding signs that read: "The people have spoken—all five of them," "Hail to the Thief," "Crime Scene," and harking back to 1960s protests, "Hey Dubya, What do you say, / How many votes did you steal today?"

Both sides continue to dispute the election. Many Democrats believe the voting irregularities point to a stolen election, while many Republicans feel that the newscasters' premature call for Gore kept some Florida Republicans from going to the polls. The most traumatic aspect for a large number of Americans was the realization that votes often go uncounted—because voting machines malfunction, voters fail to punch through their ballots forcefully enough, or from some other random cause—with potentially major consequences in a close election. Postmortems following the event included sharp criticism of the process itself and demands for mechanical improvements.

Latte Liberals and Wingnuts

Until the late twentieth century, *liberal* was a descriptive term for someone who favors government action to solve communal problems. Beginning in the late 1980s, conservatives made a practice of treating the word as a pejorative. Earlier opponents of liberalism had sometimes paired it with adjectives such as *bleeding heart* and *knee-jerk* to suggest that liberal positions were based on emotions. In the 1980s, critics took a different approach with contemptuous (usually alliterative) phrases such as *latte liberal, limousine liberal,* and *Lexus liberal.*

These labels implied that although liberals espoused populist views, they were cultural elitists, out of touch with regular folks. Similar to the early twentieth century's *parlor pink* (see Chapter 4), these terms convey the notion that liberals talk the talk while enjoying comforts like fancy coffee drinks and upscale cars.

Soon, left-leaning politicians were avoiding what became known as the L-word. During the 1988 campaign Bush joked about his opponent's refusal to own up to the "L-word label." When Dukakis finally did make a statement declaring himself a liberal in the tradition of Roosevelt, Truman, and Kennedy, the *Boston Globe* featured it as headline news: "Dukakis Uses L-Word." Liberals began adopting *progressive* as a preferred term.

In the mid-1990s *wingnut* was invented to insult those on the other end of the political spectrum—short for *right-wing nut*. Like latte liberals, wingnuts are assigned a range of stereotypical features, such as a tendency to listen to right-wing talk radio programs while driving their gun-rack-equipped pickup trucks to antigovernment rallies. *Wingnut* is also occasionally used to describe someone who is nutty in areas other than politics.

2004

GEORGE W. BUSH (REPUBLICAN) VS. JOHN KERRY (DEMOCRAT)

Swift Boating

In 2004 *swift boat* replaced *Willie Hortonize* as a synonym for a vicious personal attack on a candidate. The Swift Boat, technically known as a PCF (for Patrol Craft Fast), was a fifty-foot vessel used to patrol Vietnam's rivers and coastal waters during the war. Massachusetts senator John Kerry, the 2004 Democratic presidential candidate, commanded one such craft. During that time he was awarded three purple hearts, a silver star, and a bronze star.

A political action committee (PAC) named Swift Boat Veterans for Truth, who opposed Kerry's run for the presidency, ran a series of television ads attacking his Vietnam service. They charged that he lied about his activities there and claimed that he did not deserve his medals. They also condemned the antiwar statements that Kerry made when he returned to the United States. The group was largely financed by Republican donors.

Like the Dukakis campaign in 1988, the Kerry campaign was slow to swing into action against the ads. Eventually Kerry began speaking out. He angrily accused his opponent, President Bush, of using the group as a front "to do his dirty work." He challenged Bush—who served in the Texas Air National Guard during the war—to a comparison of records. The Bush campaign insisted that they would never question Kerry's war service, but they also refrained from condemning "the Swift Boat ads."

Most members of the Swift Boat Veterans' group had not served with Kerry. Several men who were present when Kerry won his medals came forward to deny the group's charges. One related how Kerry had saved his life under fire. The Kerry campaign also posted official navy records to contradict the Swift Boaters' claims. As with most rebuttals, Kerry's actions did not have as forcible an impact as the original attacks.

The Swift Boat attacks were not the only negative campaigning going on. A fake photograph that circulated on the Internet showed Kerry with anti–Vietnam War activist Jane Fonda at an antiwar rally. The Republicans also branded Kerry a flip-flopper because he voted to allow the use of force against Iraq in 2003, but later voted against additional funding for the Iraq War effort.

Bush's opponents also threw a few fistfuls of mud. Pro-Kerry organizations sent around emails claiming that Bush would reinstate the military draft if reelected, although no evidence suggested that he was planning such a move. When a number of people who watched the candidates' first debate noticed an apparent bulge beneath Bush's suit jacket, stories began circulating that he was wired to receive help with answers—the implication being that Bush was not smart enough to handle Kerry on his own. The White House reported that the bulge was nothing more than a wrinkle in the fabric, but some viewers remained skeptical.

Although the controversies of 2004 faded soon after the election, the term *swift boat* lives on, now transformed into a verb. One of the earliest uses in print appeared in Frank Rich's *New York Times* column for August 23, 2005, titled "The Swift Boating of Cindy Sheehan." In his piece about anti–Iraq War activist Sheehan, Rich used the term as a synonym for character assassination. Future political campaigns would fling charges and countercharges of swift boating at the first hint of negativity.

Truth Deficit

Just as President Johnson suffered from a credibility gap, later administrations were burdened with a truth deficit—the public perception that they were being less than completely frank about the facts. Republicans first used the phrase to attack President Clinton. For instance, according to newspaper reports on October 1, 1998, "GOP national committee chairman Jim Nicholson declared that Clinton was operating at a 'truth deficit' by claiming credit for the surplus." Democrats later used the term against

George W. Bush, as in this newspaper story for April 16, 2004: "John Kerry told students . . . that the president is misleading Americans about tax policies . . . and accused Mr. Bush of 'a big truth deficit.'"

A related term that burst into the limelight in 2005 was *truthiness*, a previously obscure word popularized by Stephen Colbert, host of Comedy Central's *Colbert Report*. Colbert explained in an interview, truthiness "is sort of what you want the truth to be, as opposed to what the facts support." He introduced the word with cable news commentators in mind. Both *truthiness* and *truth deficit* are still used, usually in connection with politics.

Billary

In 2008 Hillary Rodham Clinton became the first wife of a former president to run for the same office herself. She also became the first woman with a serious chance of capturing the top spot on her party's presidential ticket. Her candidacy inspired new and original forms of mudslinging.

Opponents resurrected *Billary*, a blend of *Bill* and *Hillary*. The nickname was coined during Bill Clinton's presidency to suggest that Mrs. Clinton was too involved in her husband's administration. In 2008 it implied the opposite—that ex-President Clinton would inappropriately influence his wife if she were elected. Rumors spread that he would hold a cabinet post or that the two would conduct a "co-presidency."

Clinton's early position as the Democratic frontrunner also triggered an onslaught of abuse from Republicans, many of whom had hostility left over from the days when Clinton was First Lady. Lapel buttons, T-shirts, and bumper stickers proliferated, with messages ranging from the basic—"Stop Hillary"—to the frankly misogynistic—"Stop mad cow."

Clinton was subjected to a plethora of gender-based commentary, much of it incorporated in regular news reports. The National Organization of Women's Media Hall of Shame highlighted dozens of examples, including press discussions of her laugh, her pantsuits, her purported shrillness, and an extended debate over whether she had shown too much cleavage during a Senate floor speech.

At their extreme, the attacks were remarkably ugly. Right-wing commentators habitually referred to Clinton with gender-related epithets, of which "she-devil" is probably the politest. She was described as "castrating, overbearing, and scary." Speculation that she had undergone plastic surgery competed with comments that she was looking old. When Clinton supporters accused the news media of showing a sexist bias, some journalists countered that the Clinton campaign was playing the gender card. This type of "bias" versus "bias card" exchange would become routine during the general election campaign.

Although Clinton ultimately lost the nomination to Illinois senator Barack Obama, she set a historic precedent. She won a number of major primaries and garnered nearly half the Democratic Party's pledged delegates.

2008

BARACK OBAMA (DEMOCRAT) VS. JOHN MCCAIN (REPUBLICAN)

Nobama vs. McSame

Many observers of the 2008 presidential election complained that it was just one big mudslide. This perception was no doubt partly caused by the saturation coverage, both over the airwaves and on the Internet. Besides the usual television attack ads—and with campaign spending at close to $1 billion there were plenty of them—anyone with a website, blog, or YouTube account could add a fresh dollop of slime to the mix.

Another reason why the negativity seemed to rocket to new levels may have concerned the identities of the candidates. The Democrats chose Barack Obama, the first African American to be nominated by a major party. The Republicans nominated Arizona senator John McCain, who at seventy-two would be the oldest first-term president if elected. Racist and ageist attacks were thus added to the usual negative toolkit. So were charges of racism and ageism, followed by countercharges of playing the racism or ageism card.

Negative T-shirts, buttons, bumper stickers, posters, and lawn signs were widely available. Anti-Obama paraphernalia ran the gamut from *Obama* with a "forbidden" symbol superimposed to pictures of chimpanzees and other racist imagery. *Nobama*, invented by Clinton supporters during the primaries, was also popular. Anti-McCain material emphasized his age—"No Country for Old Men" (the title of a Cormac McCarthy novel and 2007 movie)—or his connection to President George W. Bush—"McBush."

The campaigns themselves engaged in various kinds of attacks. The McCain campaign criticized Obama as a liberal elitist, out of touch with regular Americans. They underlined this message with television ads claiming that Obama was in favor of comprehensive sex education for kindergartners (he supported a bill to teach about inappropriate touching) and saying that he wanted to raise taxes on middle-class Americans (he proposed a tax raise for those with annual incomes of over $250,000).

Obama's supporters saw many of the attacks on him as coded racism. He was said to look foreign and his birthplace of Hawaii was described as outside the "real"—that is, continental—United States. A congratulatory fist bump that he exchanged with his wife, Michelle, was interpreted as having radical leftist, or "terrorist," overtones. In one news story, Fox News oddly labeled Michelle Obama his "baby mama," street slang implying that the Obamas had children together, but were not married or otherwise committed.

McCain supporters also took advantage of the uproar that arose during the primary season when videotapes surfaced of Obama's former pastor Jeremiah Wright criticizing the United States in ways that many listeners deemed anti-white. The controversy died down somewhat after Obama made a televised speech on race in which he addressed Wright's comments. McCain himself refrained from raising the issue during the campaign, but the topic remained alive and virulent in cyberspace.

In spite of the publicity surrounding Obama's pastor, rumors persisted that he was a Muslim (obviously not in itself a slur, but a negative trait to those spreading the tale). Republican speech-makers frequently referred to Obama by his full name, Barack Hussein Obama, to highlight his Muslim-sounding middle name. Emails circulated warning that Obama was a Muslim stealth candidate. Just as Franklin Roosevelt and Adlai Stevenson were attacked in the 1950s for being the preferred candidates of the Soviet Union, Obama was now labeled the preferred choice of radical Islamic terrorists.

Obama paraphrased these attacks as "he's not patriotic enough. He's got a funny name . . . he doesn't look like all those other presidents on those dollar bills." The McCain campaign promptly complained that Obama was playing the race card.

If Obama was too different, McCain was portrayed as being not different enough. President Bush's popularity had fallen sharply since his reelection, due to setbacks in Iraq and Afghanistan and economic problems at home. The Obama campaign capitalized on this situation to link McCain with Bush. Obama pointed out that McCain voted with Bush 90 percent of the time. A group called Campaign to Defend America ran an ad calling McCain the "McSame as Bush." (The trend of using *Mc* to cheapen an item, as in *McMansion*, added punch to the attack.) "McSame" and "No third term for Bush" began appearing on bumper stickers and posters.

Obama supporters obliquely suggested that McCain was too old to be president. One ad featuring a close-up of McCain's scar from recent melanoma surgery asked, "Why won't John McCain release his medical records?" (McCain's doctors gave him a clean bill of health at the start of the campaign.) Other ads used his admitted unfamiliarity with email to suggest that he was out of touch with modern technology and perhaps too old to learn.

Asked about McCain's statements that the militant Palestinian group Hamas was hoping Obama would be elected, Obama answered that such comments were "an example of him losing his bearings." This remark triggered another exchange of charges and countercharges. McCain adviser Mark Salter castigated Obama for using the expression *lose his bearings* as a "not particularly clever" way to refer to McCain's age. An Obama spokesman retorted that Obama had obviously been referring to McCain's moral compass, adding that Salter's response clearly indicated that "losing one's bearings has no relation to age."

Both campaigns misrepresented the other's position on the Iraq War. McCain ads clipped an Obama statement so that he seemed to be saying that American troops were "just air-raiding villages and killing civilians." A narrator then characterized his remarks as dangerous and dishonorable. (Obama had actually been calling for more funding and reinforcements.) The Obama campaign quoted McCain's answer to a town hall participant out of context to claim that McCain favored fighting "a one-hundred-year" war in Iraq. (He had been suggesting a Korea-like noncombat arrangement.)

As the election came down to the wire, the negative rhetoric intensified. Republican vice presidential candidate Sarah Palin repeatedly misquoted Obama's Iraq statement during speeches to accuse him of insulting the troops. She suggested that he "palled around with terrorists" based on his once sitting on a committee with former Weatherman Bill Ayers. She told audiences, "This is not a man who sees America the way you and I see America." Agitated audience members responded with shouts of "treason" and "kill him." When McCain pleaded with one crowd to be respectful, they booed.

Palin took a few knocks herself. When she had difficulty answering questions about policy issues during televised interviews, voters began questioning whether she was qualified to be vice president. Concerned Republicans called on McCain to drop her from the ticket. Her perceived shortcomings were devastatingly parodied by comedian Tina Fey on the television program *Saturday Night Live*, an image that many viewers carried with them to the polls.

In the end, the mountain of mud did not have as compelling an impact as the collapsing economy. Beginning in September, a series of Wall Street bank failures and similar business disasters triggered the worst financial crisis since the Great Depression. As usual in these situations, Americans decided that a switch of parties was in order. With the highest voter turnout in over forty years, they elected Barack Obama by a solid majority of nearly 53 percent.

Lipstick on a Pig

During her nomination acceptance speech, Sarah Palin jokingly told the Republican convention that the main difference between a hockey mom such as herself and a pit bull was lipstick. Her audience still remembered that line several days later when Barack

Obama, speaking about Republican calls for change, told the crowd, "You can put lipstick on a pig. It's still a pig." He went on to say, "You can wrap an old fish in a piece of paper called change. It's still gonna stink."

The McCain campaign immediately accused Obama of calling Palin a pig and declared their outrage at his sexist remark. The Obama campaign called the accusation absurd, saying that *lipstick on a pig* was an old, well-known idiom. They also noted that McCain himself had used the same expression the previous year to describe Hillary Clinton's healthcare proposal.

The expression *lipstick on a pig*, meaning "to dress up an idea so it appears fresher or more appealing," first arose in the 1980s. However, earlier versions of the same maxim have been around since the eighteenth century. An 1887 collection of proverbs titled *The Salt-Cellars* gives the following version: "'A hog in a silk waistcoat is still a hog,' meaning, 'Circumstances do not alter a man's nature, nor even his manners.'" Texas governor Ann Richards popularized the modern expression during the early 1990s with her frequent references to a hog decked out with lipstick and named Monique.

Getting Thrown Under the Bus

When Reverend Jeremiah Wright continued to appear on television and provide news commentators with colorful sound bites, Obama was moved to distance himself from his former pastor. He repudiated Wright's remarks during a press conference and later announced that he and his wife had resigned their membership in Wright's church. Although many commentators approved of Obama's actions, others accused the candidate of throwing his onetime friend under the bus.

Under the bus was first used in a nonpolitical context. One of its earliest print appearances is in a September 7, 1984, *Washington Post* interview with singer Cyndi Lauper by David Remnick. Remnick begins, "In the rock 'n' roll business, you are either on the bus or under it." He may have been thinking of the familiar command that sports coaches give their team when they're about to leave for the big game—be on the bus or under it. In other words, get with the program or risk being flattened. Actually getting thrown under the bus is a more brutal fate—a betrayal by a fellow team member. *Thrown under the bus* began appearing in print in the early 1990s.

When the expression popped up during the Wright controversy, news commentators embraced it. Any evidence of conflict was seen as a possible incident of flinging someone under the wheels. Linguist Geoffrey Nunberg, speaking on an April 2008 segment of National Public Radio's *Fresh Air* program, estimated that *throw under the bus* had appeared in more than four hundred press stories about the campaign.

It remains popular in political commentary circles, perhaps because it encompasses so much of what politics is about. After all, under the bus is where you find the mud.

AFTERWORD

The mudslinging tradition is still going strong after more than two hundred years of American politics. That's not surprising—electoral history shows that it works! On the other hand, those who fear for the future can take heart from the realization that at least things aren't getting worse. Even the most brutal attacks are really nothing new. From Washington's day to the present, the same tried-and-true smears have been rolled out before each election.

Consider how many presidential hopefuls contended with these perennial charges:

- ★ **ELITISM AND EGGHEADERY:** John Quincy Adams, Martin Van Buren, Adlai Stevenson, Michael Dukakis, Al Gore, and Barack Obama

- ★ **IGNORANCE AND LACK OF DIGNITY:** Andrew Jackson, William Henry Harrison, Abraham Lincoln, Warren Harding, Al Smith, and George W. Bush

- ★ **TOO RADICAL:** Thomas Jefferson, William Jennings Bryan,

Franklin Roosevelt, Barry Goldwater, George McGovern, and Barack Obama

★ **TOO HIDEBOUND:** John Adams, John Quincy Adams, James Polk, Herbert Hoover, and John McCain

★ **MENTAL INSTABILITY:** Horace Greeley, William Jennings Bryan, Barry Goldwater, and vice presidential candidate Tom Eagleton

★ **PROBLEMATIC WAR RECORD:** Andrew Jackson, William Henry Harrison, Franklin Pierce, Bill Clinton, and John Kerry

★ **WRONG RELIGION:** John Quincy Adams, William Taft, John Frémont, Al Smith, and John Kennedy

★ **ROMANTIC TROUBLES:** Andrew Jackson, Grover Cleveland, Woodrow Wilson, Warren Harding, and Bill Clinton

Charges of corruption have been leveled at too many candidates to list, starting with George Washington.

In spite of all the accusations and shouting, and threats of dire consequences should the wrong person win, new administrations continue to be peacefully sworn in every four years. That includes the years after the disputed elections of 1876 and 2000. Even during times of war and secession, elected presidents have taken office on schedule. Mudslinging is simply part of that time-honored democratic process—the American way of politics.

ACKNOWLEDGMENTS

I owe big thank-yous to the following people: Meg Leder, my editor at Perigee, for her excellent comments and suggestions, and for making the whole publishing process so smooth; copyeditor Candace B. Levy for her careful work; my agent, Janet Rosen of Sheree Bykofsky Associates, for her enthusiasm and professional support; and my longtime critique group, Mary-Kate Mackey, Sally Sheklow, and Deanna Larson, for their invaluable comments and advice.

SELECTED BIBLIOGRAPHY

Many newspaper quotations were located through the *Oxford English Dictionary* or the Newspaper Archive online. The dating of political words and expressions is based on information in the *Oxford English Dictionary* and the journal *American Speech*. Election statistics come from the *New York Times Almanac* for 2009.

Abels, Jules. *The Degeneration of Our Presidential Election*. New York: Macmillan, 1968.

Adams, Samuel Hopkins. *Incredible Era: The Life and Times of Warren Gamaliel Harding*. Boston: Houghton Mifflin, 1930.

Allen, Oliver E. *The Tiger: The Rise and Fall of Tammany Hall*. Reading, Mass.: Addison-Wesley, 1993.

Baker, Jean H. *James Buchanan*. New York: Times Books, 2004.

Barrett, Grant, ed. *Hatchet Jobs and Hardball: The Oxford Dictionary of American Political Slang*. Oxford: Oxford University Press, 2004.

Bartlett, John Russell. *Dictionary of Americanisms*. 1848. Reprint, with a foreword by Richard Lederer. Hoboken, N.J.: Wiley, 2003.

"The Battle for the Democratic Party." *Time*, July 17, 1972, p. 11–16.

Blake, Fay M., and H. Morton Newman. *Verbis Non Factis: Words Meant to Influence Political Choices in the United States, 1800–1980*. Metuchen, N.J.: Scarecrow Press, 1984.

Boller, Paul F., Jr. *Presidential Campaigns from George Washington to George W. Bush.* Oxford: Oxford University Press, 2004.

Burns, Eric. *Infamous Scribblers: The Founding Fathers and the Rowdy Beginnings of American Journalism.* New York: PublicAffairs, 2007.

Burns, James MacGregor. *Roosevelt: The Lion and the Fox.* New York: Harcourt Brace, 1956.

Byrdsall, Fitzwilliam. *The History of the Loco-Foco or Equal Rights Party.* New York: Clement & Packard, 1842.

"The Campaign in Retrospect: Long, Bitter, Wearying Fight." *Newsweek*, November 10, 1952, p. 23–31.

Childs, Marquis W. "They Hate Roosevelt." *Harper's* 172 (May 1936): 634–642.

Cooper, Michael. "On Bearings and Age." The Caucus, *New York Times*, May 9, 2008, www.nytimes.com.

Craigie, Sir William A., and James Hulbert, eds. *A Dictionary of American English on Historical Principles*, 4 vols. Chicago: University of Chicago Press, 1938–1944.

Davis, David Brion, and Steven Mintz, eds. *The Boisterous Sea of Liberty: A Documentary History from Discovery to the Civil War.* Oxford: Oxford University Press, 1998.

"Democratic Strategy for '52." *Life*, June 2, 1952, p. 30.

Denton, Robert E., Jr. ed. *The 2008 Presidential Campaign: A Communication Perspective.* Lanham, Md.: Rowman & Littlefield, 2009.

Donaldson, Gary A. *The First Modern Campaign: Kennedy, Nixon, and the Election of 1960.* Lanham, Md.: Rowman & Littlefield, 2007.

Drew, Elizabeth. *Portrait of an Election: The 1980 Presidential Campaign.* New York: Simon & Schuster, 1981.

Evjen, Henry O. "An Analysis of Some of the Propaganda Features of the Campaign of 1940." *Southwestern Social Science Quarterly* 27 (December 1946): 235–261.

Faragher, John Mack, et al. *Out of Many: A History of the American People.* Combined 2nd ed. Upper Saddle River, N.J.: Prentice-Hall, 1999.

Foner, Eric. *Give Me Liberty! An American History.* 2nd ed. New York: Norton, 2009.

Frommer, Arthur, ed. *Goldwater from A to Z: A Critical Handbook.* New York: Frommer/Pasmentier, 1964.

SELECTED BIBLIOGRAPHY

Gammon, Samuel Rhea. *The Presidential Campaign of 1832*. Baltimore: Johns Hopkins University Press, 1922.

Germond, Jack W., and Jules Witcover. *Mad as Hell: Revolt at the Ballot Box*. New York: Warner Books, 1993.

Germond, Jack W., and Jules Witcover. *Whose Broad Stripes and Bright Stars? The Trivial Pursuit of the Presidency, 1988*. New York: Warner Books, 1989.

Gould, Lewis L. *Four Hats in the Ring: The 1912 Election and the Birth of Modern American Politics*. Lawrence: University Press of Kansas, 2008.

Gould, Lewis L. *1968: The Election That Changed America*. Chicago: Ivan R. Dee, 1993.

Hesseltine, William Best. *Ulysses S. Grant: Politician*. New York: Dodd Mead, 1935.

Johnson, Haynes. *The Best of Times: America in the Clinton Years*. New York: Harcourt, 2001.

Kelly, Michael. "'Did Not' and 'Did So' Frame the Tax Debate." *New York Times*, September 1, 1992, p. A14.

Leuchtenburg, William. "The Wrong Man at the Wrong Time." *American Heritage*, May 26, 2009, www.americanheritage.com.

Lindsay, Charles. "More Political Lingo." *American Speech* 2 (July 1927): 443.

Lorant, Stefan. *The Glorious Burden: The American Presidency*. New York: Harper & Row, 1968.

Mathews, Mitford M. *A Dictionary of Americanisms on Historical Principles*, 2 vols. Chicago: University of Chicago Press, 1955.

McMaster, John Bach. *A History of the People of the United States from the Revolution to the Civil War*, 8 vols. New York: Appleton-Century, 1885–1937.

Mencken, H. L. *A Carnival of Buncombe*. Edited by Malcolm Moos. Baltimore: Johns Hopkins University Press, 1956.

Milbank, Dana. "Unleashed, Palin Makes Pit Bull Look Tame." *Washington Post*, October 7, 2008, p. A3.

Miller, Nathan. *Theodore Roosevelt: A Life*. New York: William Morrow, 1992.

Minnegerode, Meade. *Presidential Years: 1787–1860*. New York: Putnam's Sons, 1928.

Moore, Edmund G. *A Catholic Runs for President: The Campaign of 1928*. New York: Ronald Press, 1956.

"The Morality Issue." *Newsweek*, November 2, 1964, p. 25–26.

Nevins, Allan. *Grover Cleveland: A Study in Courage.* New York: Dodd Mead, 1932.

Nunberg, Geoffrey. *Talking Right.* New York: PublicAffairs, 2007.

Oberholtzer, Ellis Paxton. *A History of the United States Since the Civil War,* 5 vols. New York: Macmillan, 1917–1937.

Poore, Benjamin Perley. *Perley's Reminiscences of Sixty Years in the National Metropolis.* Philadelphia: Hubbard Bros., 1886.

"The Republican Nomination for the Presidency." *New York Herald,* May 19, 1860, p. 6.

Roberts, Robert N., and Scott J. Hammond. *Encyclopedia of Presidential Campaigns, Slogans, Issues, and Platforms.* Westport, Conn.: Greenwood Press, 2004.

Safire, William. *Safire's New Political Dictionary.* New York: Random House, 1993.

Scherer, Michael. "Race to the Bottom." *Time,* October 6, 2008, p. 46.

Schlesinger, Arthur M., Jr., ed. *History of American Presidential Elections 1789–1968,* 4 vols. New York: Chelsea House, 1971.

Schram, Martin. "The Making of Willie Horton." *New Republic,* May 28, 1990, p. 17.

Steinberg, Jacques. "Truthiness." Week in Review, *New York Times,* December 25, 2005, p. 3.

Stoddard, Henry L. *As I Knew Them: Presidents and Politics from Grant to Coolidge.* New York: Harper & Bros., 1927.

Swint, Kerwin C. *Mudslingers: The Top 25 Negative Political Campaigns of All Time.* Westport, Conn.: Praeger, 2006.

Tagg, James. *Benjamin Franklin Bache and the Philadelphia Aurora.* Philadelphia: University of Pennsylvania Press, 1991.

"Three Whispers." *Time,* September 17, 1928, p. 9.

Traister, Rebecca. "Life's a Bitch, and So Are All the Anti-Hillary Slogans." *Salon,* January 28, 2008, www.salon.com.

Washington Post Staff. *Deadlock: The Inside Story of America's Closest Election.* New York: PublicAffairs, 2001.

White, Theodore H. *The Making of the President, 1964.* New York: Atheneum, 1965.

White, Theodore H. *The Making of the President, 1972.* New York: Atheneum, 1973.

Wimberly, L. C. "Political Cant." *American Speech* 2 (December 1926): 135–139.

INDEX

INDEX

changeover after election, 47–48
Chase, Salmon, 50
Chicago riots, 132, 151–52, 153
Chicago Times-Herald, 82
Chicago Tribune, 111, 116, 129
chicken hawks, 174–75
Chinook Jargon, 28
Choice (film), 148
Christian Science Monitor, 125, 139
Cicero, 146
Cincinnati Enquirer, 99
Cincinnati Gazette, 6
citizenship for African Americans, 51
Civil Service, 55, 56, 59
Civil War, 26, 27, 42–44, 48, 50, 52, 79
   See also Antebellum Period and the
     Civil War (1852–1868)
Clay, Henry
   1824 (Democratic-Republican), xi,
     2–4, 87
   1832 (National Republican), 8, 10–11
   1844 (Whig), 21–22
Cleveland, Grover
   1884 (Democrat), 52, 53, 64–69, 88,
     123
   1888 (Democrat), 70–72
   1892 (Democrat), 72–73
Clinton, Bill
   1992 (Democrat), 180, 182–87
   1996 (Democrat), 182, 188–89, 196,
     197
Clinton, Hillary, 184, 189, 197–98, 204
coat-holders, 125–26
*Col. Crockett's Exploits and Adventures in
   Texas* (Crockett), 14
Colbert, Stephen, 197
Cold War, 137
Columbus Dispatch, 69
Commie Symps, 138
Committee to Re-Elect the President
   (CREEP), 162–63
Commoner, 88

communism, 80, 96, 116, 124–25, 131,
   133–34, 137–40
Compromise of 1850, 30–31, 32
Confederate Army, 42–43, 50, 57
Congressional Globe, 15, 39, 47
Congressional Record, 63, 91, 115
Congress of Industrial Organizations (CIO)
   Political Action Committee, 123
Connecticut Courant, ix
Conscience Whigs (Woolly Whigs, Black
   Republicans), 42
Constitutional Union Party (Do-Nothings),
   41–42
   See also Bell, John
contraction vs. imperialism, 79
cookie pushers, 126–27
Coolidge, Calvin 1924 (Republican),
   100–102, 105
Copperheads (Peace Democrats), 43, 48, 49
corrupt bargain, 2–4
Cotton Whigs (Silver Grays), 42
Coughlin, Father Charles, 115
Cox, James 1920 (Democrat), 20, 97–99,
   100, 110
Crawford, William 1824 (Democratic-
   Republican), xi, 2–4, 87
credibility gap, 148–49, 196
Crédit Mobilier scandal, 55, 63, 64
Crockett, David, 12, 14
Cuomo, Mayor, 126

Daily Telegram (Nebraska), 145
Daisy Ad, 146–47
Daley, Richard, 144, 151, 152, 153
Davis, Jefferson, 57
Davis, John 1924 (Democrat), 100–102,
   105
debates, 143–44, 152, 169–70, 179–80,
   183, 196
Debs, Eugene 1912 (Socialist), 89–93
debunk, 9
Defiance Democrat, 58–59

INDEX

INDEX

INDEX